The Eye Aware

The Eye Aware
Zen Lessons for Christians

❧

Jeroen Witkam

Lantern Books • New York
A Division of Booklight Inc.

2001
Lantern Books
One Union Square West, Suite 201
New York, NY 10003

Copyright © Jeroen Witkam 2001

Biblical quotations are, with a few exceptions, taken from the New Jerusalem Bible (New York: Doubleday, 1990).

This book was published in 1992 by Lannoo Uitgeverij NV in Belgium and the Netherlands under the title, *Het Geopende Oog*, and translated by Oscar and Robbert Schrover in 1999.

Printed in the United States of America

Library of Congress Cataloging-in-Publication Data

Witkam, Jeroen
   The eye aware / Jeroen Witkam
      p. cm.
   ISBN 1-930051-04-2
     1. Spiritual life—Christianity. 2. Spiritual life—Zen Buddhism. 3. Zen Buddhism—Relations—Christianity. 4. Christianity and other religions—Zen Buddhism. I. Title.

BV4501.3.W58 2001
248.3—dc21

2001029891

Table of Contents

Introduction

FOR MORE THAN TWENTY YEARS, A GROUP OF fellow monks, visitors, and I have been organizing Zen sessions at our Abbey Maria Toevlucht or "Mary's Refuge," situated in the vicinity of the little village of Zundert near the old city of Breda in the Netherlands. Our particular aim has been to integrate Zazen into the life of Christian prayer. We were greatly inspired to do this by Karlfried Graf Dürckheim and Father Hugo Enomiya-Lassalle, who both died not long ago, and to whom we are greatly beholden.

Some time ago, in a small book entitled *Guarding Your Heart*, I tried to shed some light on our intentions and the background of these explorations into Zen. Just as the Church Fathers sought to integrate Platonism into Christianity and Saint Thomas Aquinas extended these efforts towards Aristotelianism, so it seemed our genuine calling to find a niche for the study and contemplation of the Eastern ways of boundless concentration. *The Eye Aware* is an attempt to expound this goal.

Most of the time, short discourses were held during our countless Zen sessions. These sessions were not intended to provide us with material for contemplation, but to be affirmations or arrows to help the practitioner find the target. Hoping to attain this goal, we always drew upon the Scriptures. We took our ways of sitting and breathing from the tradition of Zazen—an emptying of consciousness and the attainment of a transparent heart-mind, which mirrors the paths of inwardness that exist in all truly great spiritual traditions. On the path to true inwardness, according to the method of Zazen, the Bible proved to be an excellent source of inspiration. It did not offer us any methodology, but instead offered countless and, above all, diverse images. While enormously varied, these images were interwoven with consistent elements from the tradition of Zazen. We sat, breathed, and fostered a silenced consciousness. We tried to create an awareness that is a void yet not empty, one that, in a very gradual manner, becomes an overflowing state of fullness and, above all, state of compassion.

This book does not seek to supply the reader with a simple system of edification, but rather to present him or her with images taken from the Bible that may take him or her into a stream or "flowing forth" of awareness. Let the reader not forget that meditation always means starting from scratch, beginning anew.

This book is a result of a communal effort, the afterglow of a spiritual adventure by like-minded friends—both monks and visitors to the Abbey alike. It is the result of all those who urged me to publish this material, sections of which had previously been *[handwritten annotation in top margin: what one does intuitively (in the right mind) is closest to being with God]*

published in various magazines. I would like to thank these people, and above all the deep silence, which, as it turned out, constituted a form of non-verbal communication, an intense and intuitive contact. Over the years, the accumulating half-hourly sessions began to reflect our ideals much better. For example, our noisy alarm clock, that went off after every thirty-minute session, was replaced with a silent, flickering, digital device.

For myself, I want to say that in all these years two things have securely lodged in my heart: first, that the dimension of consciousness that unfolds through Zazen has been engulfed by the love of the self-revealing God. And, secondly, I believe that an extended survey of these dimensions of consciousness will eventually lead to a more fruitful dialogue between Christian and East Asian religions—not as some kind of word game, but as a powerful experiential force.

[handwritten annotation in left margin: in this state of mind - God reveals more of himself to us]

Finally, I would like to add a gentle word of warning: This is not a book to rush through. Every part demands its own pace, and requires attention, ample time, and tranquility so its message may sink in slowly.

❦

1. The Fish Becomes a Dragon

IN WESTERN EUROPE, AND ALSO IN AMERICA, AN increasing number of people are practicing Zazen or Zen meditation. In turn, Japanese Buddhists are eagerly observing Christianity, wondering how it will cope with the challenges of a modern, secularized society. Actually, these Buddhists admire how positively the Catholic Church took up these challenges after the Second Vatican Council. As a result, there has arisen a mutual desire among Christians and Zen Buddhists to get to know each other better.

Why do Christians put their mind to Zen meditation? And why do they want to start a dialogue with Buddhism?

I can well imagine some people saying that Christianity is altogether unique, and that Jesus Himself is the unique Way and Door to salvation. Buddhists, these people retort, simply have to become Christians. Yet, I believe strongly that there is another, third option, and this possibility is what I will try to outline.

People often proclaim: "We Christians have our own mystical tradition—one so immensely profuse and overpowering that there is simply no cause for any of us to take an active interest in the mystical paths of other religions. What, in Heaven's name, could they bring us?"

Yet it is a fact that, in the wake of the profound secularism that has corroded modern Christianity, a spiritual hunger has emerged seeking inspiration and direction, and it is focused upon the Asian traditions. Why, in spite of the genuine spiritual hunger, this breeze did not come to rest on the vast lake of Christian tradition is a very complex phenomenon. Nevertheless, I would like to point out at least one possible reason.

In our artificial, technocratic, and urbanized society, modern human beings have lost touch with their own bodies. Despite our vast treasure of scientific medical knowledge in the West, we don't know what to do with our physicality. The body as a vehicle for experience or perception, as an instrument for detecting oneself, has become a foreign object.

The most striking characteristic of Buddhist and Hindu mysticism is that they commence with the body. Christianity, on the other hand, has always begun with the Word, a living word from God, which embraced humankind wholly and placed it in the grand tide of history. But the increasingly rationalized, scientifically developed human being is only able to approach Christianity rationally. With the disappearance of physical awareness, a lot of emotions and processes have been lost and have become inaccessible to our culture.

Seen from this perspective it is not surprising that the renewed spiritual hunger that has revealed itself in the West has turned eastward in an effort to learn from its ancient wisdom of body-awareness, and to tap into new sources of experiences that

6

have been lost to the West. Christians, and especially the clergy, who felt their experience of the Divine had become too rigid to continue, uncovered a new impulse in the Eastern ways of meditation, a new way of gaining awareness that would bring life to the Christian tradition.

Although at times the various forms of Hindu Yoga are spiritually very one-sided and extremely complicated, the Buddhist way of Zazen is surprising because of its simplicity and directness. The Zen tradition has, more than other Eastern traditions, preserved its contact with daily life. That is why many people, and many Christians too, feel attracted to the simplicity of the path of Zazen.

What is Zazen? = meditation

Zazen is a form of objectless or imageless meditation. The Christian tradition is very familiar with objectless meditation: Just think, for example, of the exhortations of Saint John of the Cross, mystics to whom objectless awareness was the result of a prolonged and intensified communion with biblical words and images that, after a while, became stilled into pure "thusness," most appropriately described as a transparent state of Presence. Zazen has another starting-point. It begins with our own body.

A correct bearing is a precondition of reaching pure natural breathing, a pure breath-consciousness. The correct bearing is, simply stated, sitting erect. This is not done by pushing one's shoulders up. On the contrary, it really takes place when you sink into your pelvis, and find—as they say in Japanese—*hara*. Hara is a force, a kind of energy-center, located in the subtle body around the belly, just a few fingers under the navel. There, you have to open the upward-striving forces that enable you to sit erect without any obvious strain to the body.

It sounds very simple to talk about just sitting erect. But, because we have become estranged from our bodies, sitting erect is very hard in reality. It demands quite a lot of practice to learn it, yet it is a good way to get into the swing of your own body. Of course, much more can be said about this topic, but I want to confine myself to a more concise description of what actually matters.

❮ A correct posture is obviously a precondition for breathing properly. It is also a conscious way of getting familiar with your own breath. To the East Asian religions, breath is always the mediating influence that provides us with a proper experience of spiritual reality. Indeed, the same applies to the Bible. If you're in doubt, just read the passage in which Jesus speaks to Nicodemus about the necessity of being born anew. Rebirth occurs through the Spirit, but in Greek and in Hebrew the term "spirit" is synonymous with breath and wind. Jesus also refers to the secret of the wind, while at Whitsun He breathes upon his pupils, before saying: "Receiveth thou the Holy Spirit."

❮ After right bearing and proper breathing, the third step in Zazen is correct consciousness—an awareness no longer curbed by images and desires. In Japanese Zen monasteries, practitioners endlessly recite the so-called "Heart Sutra," the *hanyo shingyo*. The Heart Sutra has a singular refrain: "Form is emptiness, emptiness is form." In an existential analysis, this sutra attempts to show us that reality is essential empty, from which it follows that all our fears are only illusions.

Let me summarize this shortly in my own words: All objects possess form and shape. We say, for example, that a doormat is rectangular and a cushion is round. We attribute certain properties or a quality to the mat and a cushion, and we do this by using a copula or verb-link, such as the word "is." This copula seems so unimportant that several languages omit the word. And yet it has a profound meaning, because before we can establish that the mat is square and the cushion round, we say the mat is there or the cushion is there. The mat exists, the cushion exists.

This declaration is the most essential thing you can say of anything, and yet at the same time the declaration is completely empty. When you claim that something exists—that it "is"—you are not imagining its reality. It is impossible to define "is" as one form since it contains all possible forms—"is" has countless possibilities. When, in a Zen monastery, the monks say "form is emptiness, emptiness is form," they want to give us an awareness of that pure, undiluted state of being that precedes any form. Moreover, when we enter the state of silence during Zen meditation, and put our minds to Zazen, we begin to shape this formula into a realized, instantaneous awareness.

Once we have learned to adopt the proper posture and practiced proper breathing, it is necessary for us to confront our daily stream of images—those pictures and compelling scenes and sequences that pass our mind's eye as if they were filmed. Often these mental images are primarily borrowed from our immediate surroundings, but through the practice of Zazen these images gradually incorporate sights from forgotten yesterdays, pictures we no longer remember or tend to overlook because we feel they are no longer of any importance to us. Zen tradition gives a very simple instruction about how we may handle this phenomenon: We are told not to entertain these images. We are not to suppress them violently, but to let them flow by, gently. Zen teaches us to try, time and again, to reach that state of boundless awareness and emptiness.

In Japan, referring to Mount Fuji, a famous, solitary, high rising peak in the Bay of Tokyo, they say: "Sit in meditation as Mount Fuji." The clouds—your thoughts—let them pass. Simply let them float by. You must only sit still. Like Mount Fuji.

* * *

What happens when you turn toward the emptiness of the consciousness is that you get in touch with the deepest level of being, with your own singular essence, a "suchness" that is inexplicable, unfathomable, and yet fundamental. The proper source of being, of "thusness," is also a source of beauty. When, after having sat in the silence of Zazen for a while, you stand up and look about you, you notice that everything has acquired its original, innate splendor and beauty again. Your perception has been cleansed and changed and has opened up to the Infinite.

After we practice the basic exercise "form is emptiness," we discover that emptiness always takes shape again, but that the form has been set free from its self-encasement. It has opened up to its original source. Lao Tzu, a Chinese sage from the sixth century BCE, who considerably influenced the Zen tradition in Japan and China, expressed this most eloquently in one of his sayings.

Thirty spokes share the wheel's hub;
It is the center hole that makes it useful.
Shape clay into a vessel,
it is the space that makes it useful;
cut doors and windows for a room,
it is the holes which make it useful.
Therefore profit comes from what is not there.[1]

You will find similar thoughts and views in the Bible, too. When Jesus seeks to explain the mysterious, unfathomable ascent of the kingdom of God, He lists how human beings have involved themselves in all sorts of practices that make up their daily routine: eating, drinking, marrying, giving into matrimony, buying and selling, building and planting. Yet this entire chain of events is humanity's doom, just as it came to pass in the days of Noah and Lot. But those with a watchful, discerning eye, looking for the kingdom of God, Jesus says, will be saved. (Luke 17:27–30)

Paul asserts the same thing, although somewhat differently. He describes similar processes, and admonishes human beings not to let themselves to be defined by them: "Those who have wives," he elaborates, "should live as though they had none; and those who have been buying property as though they had no possessions." Moreover, Paul adds psychological qualities: "Those who mourn, [should live] as though they were not mourning; and

---

[1.] Lao Tzu, *Tao te Ching* translated by Gia Fu Feng and Jane English (London: Wildwood House, 1973).

those who enjoy life as though they did not enjoy it." Why? Because time is short.

Paul falls back here on the established eschatological perspective of the Bible. But what he really wants to say is that every form, every sociological process and psychological constitution, is essentially empty. "And those who are involved with the world [should live] as though they were people not engrossed in it. Because this world as we know it is passing away." (1 Cor. 7:25–31)

Zazen is a very deep and radical process. It is not without reason that Zen monks refer to this process with the formula, "Dying the Great Death." In view of the transient nature of their existence, human beings, when facing death, experience the innermost values of their life, and in front of them opens a road that leads them into the light. If, for the Buddhist, the road into the light signifies the pristine unity of everything that exists, what does this signify for the Christian?

The Christian knows himself to be stirred by the word of the self-revealing God. He experiences being addressed individually, something that makes him grasp that in order to gain admission to God's Heart of Hearts, he also must die. He must die the death of Christ that those who follow Him need to share with Him, too.

⟨ For Christians, the significance of Zazen is as follows. Zazen can help the Christian unfold the depths of his existence to the voice of God, the God who loves him. It may help him absorb the words of the Bible not merely on verbal or rational grounds, but by using it to fill up the vital sources of his life.

* * *

Form is emptiness, emptiness is form. In Europe, the knowledge of Zen is often restricted to Zazen, to silent meditation. Should you go to Japan, however, you'll be surprised to learn how much of the Zen experience of emptiness has taken shape in the various levels of Japanese culture. You will find Zen in the rites of the monastery, in the beauty of the Zen garden, in the refined esthetics of the tea ceremony, and in the enormous power behind the cultivation of the various martial arts. You may also encounter Zen in daily life. Zen, after all, is doing normal things with a pure and undivided attention. As writer Karlfried Graf Dürckheim stated: "Our daily life is our exercise." It is about attention: When we sit we should sit, we should walk when we walk, and when we make our bed we should not think about the newspaper we want to read afterwards.

The Christian tradition also emphasizes that no matter what your experience of God might have been, it all boils down to living unobtrusively—the seemingly uneventful days of daily practice and the performance of small acts.

What is the best description for the emptiness of Zazen? I believe the most adequate expression for Zazen is the one I just mentioned: "Dying the Great Death." Its emptiness is so sweeping that one can speak of Zazen as a dying experience. It is not the physical demise we know of and may observe from close proximity, but it is the *inner* death that has been proclaimed by all great mystics. Emptying your mind culminates in the loss of self, which is experienced as "dying."

For the Zen Buddhist, the point of "dying" is *satori* or illumination. It is a burst, a breakthrough into the light. Zen is part of a greater Buddhist tradition commonly referred to as

"Mahayana" (literally "the Great Vehicle," or that which holds everything), whose main characteristics are an attitude of compassion and mildness toward everything that exists. The ideal figure within the Mahayana tradition is the Bodhisattva. The Bodhisattva has received illumination and is fit to enter *Nirvana*, the blissful unity in which human beings are freed from all their sufferings. She or he, however, refuses to go, and instead dedicates him- or herself to the redemption of creation. The solemn promise of the Bodhisattva is recited daily in the Zen temples: "Regardless of the countless number of beings, I promise to save them all."

Is Zazen a purely personal way? It certainly seems that way. And yet over-personalization is something that is strongly condemned by Zen tradition. From the outset, the intention of Zazen is to introduce you to an all-embracing compassion and a universal mildness. Remarkably, in the vow spoken by the Bodhisattva, both savior and pupil speak concurrently: "Despite the number of my passions and delusions, I promise to still them. Irrespective of the number of *Dharma* teachings and cosmic wisdom, I promise to master them." In these latter two affirmations the pupil is speaking—and the path of the pupil is ultimately the way of self-sacrificial compassion.

Each and every one of the Zen monks I have met in Japan were, to my mind, people with an exceeding mildness, in whose warmth you could really feel at home. Mildness and compassion are also a fundamental aspect of the experience of emptiness. And we might add a third aspect, namely the element of force. It demands enormous energy to withstand the unceasing flow of

images. What I mean by this I can best explain with a symbol—
the image of a dragon.

The Dragon

As opposed to Western fairy tales and, for that matter, biblical
metaphors, in which the dragon is the symbol of the destructive
forces of existence, the Chinese and Japanese traditions perceive
the dragon as a symbol of vigor. In most temples you see the
dragon pictured on a wall or the ceiling of a sacred space. A
familiar expression in Zen tradition runs as follows: "At the
dragon gate the fish becomes a dragon."

Imagine yourself to be the Yellow River, breaking through
the massive rock formations, splashing and thundering through a
small ravine. At the bottom of the waterfall are quiet, murky
waters, where fish thrive and swim in the still, muddy ponds. But
there are also fish that generate such a force in themselves that
they are able to overcome the waterfall. They swim against the
stream of ideas and images.

It really demands the utmost effort to reach a state of image-
lessness and not be swept along. These fish develop bulging eyes,
acquire horns on their heads, and start to grow more and more
frightening in appearance, until they gradually become dragons.
The closer they approach the inner stillness, the greater their force
becomes, as does their ability to defy the thundering violence of
the water. They swim against the stream and, by the time the
stillness is perfect and they have landed on top of the waterfall,
these fish have become dragons. It is at *that* moment that the
expression heard so often in Zen tradition applies to them:
"Buddha, that is you."

When this happens in Zen practice, you have broken through into the spiritual dimension of your existence. A vigor and essence develop within you. You no longer know fear and are able to endure everything. There is light, compassion, and force, and the emptiness has grown fertile.

2. *The Body in the Story of Creation*

I T IS PERHAPS STRANGE TO COMPARE THE JUDEO-
Christian creation story with Zen. Yet, I believe such a
comparison makes sense, because Zen is something deeply
common to all humankind. Even though Zen came from Asia and
developed in a culture totally different from Western culture, the
reason we practice it in the West is that we have learned to value
its humanity, as something through which we may expand our
human nature. In that sense, it shouldn't surprise us that we can
perceive the story of creation in the light of Zen. Genesis, in turn,
not only reveals to us something about Zen but, indeed,
something about Zen meditation.

What I have in mind is the so-called second creation myth, in
which creation is represented in only one small sentence: "The
Lord formed man from the dust of the earth. He blew into his
nostrils the breath of life, and man became a living being." (Gen.
2:7) There are precisely two elements that enable us to deal with
this matter at greater length: "The Lord formed Man from the
dust of the earth," and "He blew into his nostrils the breath of

life." In this chapter I will deal only with the first section of this verse.

The soil described in the first section of the verse is not merely sand one can simply blow away. That would hardly have been God's intention, since it would have been impossible to form anything with such insubstantial material. What is really meant here is mire, the kind of muddy clay soil used by a potter. The Hebrew term for the word can be translated as "forming" or "modeling"—words that remind us of an artist who, by means of modeling, is expressing something.

On first blush, this modeling appears a self-contained symbol, one that neatly represents the event of creation, telling us how Man owes his origin to God. But let's go a bit deeper into the substance of this symbol. Does the symbol merely establish the fact that Man is made by God? Why is an image, a symbol, being used? And, we can ask: Once the purpose of the symbol has been ascertained, will all the meaning of this sentence be satisfied, or does the word "modeling"—forming the earth, shaping the body—tell us something more?

The Force of Touch

Modeling is done with the hands and fingers; it is a mode of touching. If we think of modeling in this way, our feeling for what modeling may mean becomes more tangible, mainly because we can sense more completely what human touch may involve. For example, when a child has never been cuddled, caressed, or touched by its mother, it suffers serious psychological damage. A child that never has been touched finds it very difficult to thrive. In other words, caressing, being touched by your mother, being cuddled, are modes of giving life, bestowing an identity, and imparting self-realization.

We know this is not just relevant to the relationship between a child and its mother. One way or another, human contact—even only a simple handshake—plays a significant role in every human relationship. What the touch represents is the meaning that other person has for me, or I for that person. Touching creates a relationship, endowing the other with a form of identity that is experienced within the relationship. At the same time, touching is a way of modeling—the other person becomes him- or herself in and through that touch.

This interaction takes place in every human relationship; and that relationship becomes a form of continuing creation. Mankind continues what originally transpired during Creation— the body is formed, the physique is modeled. Thus, creation is not only something that occurred as a singular event in the past, it is also located here and now, and is continued in the present. Modeling shows that the statement, "The Lord formed Man from the dust of the earth," is not just an image, a symbol illustrating an abstraction—that Man is created by God—but it is something that expresses something larger, namely what is actually taking place right now, through the human touch.

To my mind, something similar happens in Zen meditation. Actually, it is not specific to Zen meditation, but occurs in all the forms of bodily awareness that have come to us from the Asian religions. This is especially the case in all sorts of meditation practice in which an awareness of the body plays a substantial role.

To be aware of our bodies does not mean we're just gaining awareness of the body, but that we're becoming aware of our body as some kind of essential experience, an experience of "thusness." Whenever we adopt the proper physical posture, God, as it were, is modeling our body. Let's examine this statement more closely.

As I mentioned previously, when we practice Zen meditation, we pay a great deal of particular attention to the right posture, the idea being to foster awareness of our body. Because of the entire pattern of our civilization, we Westerners have become extremely detached from our bodies. We really don't know what to do with them; our limbs just seem to dangle about us. This lack of bodily awareness indicates that we're also suffering from a partial loss of identity. The Asian forms of meditation have actually been given to us in such a way that we can obtain a better body-awareness, especially as a mode of self-discovery. Through them we can discover our very essence. In that regard, it's perhaps odd that the body for us is the thing most estranged from us.

Now, while scientifically we know everything about the body since science has disclosed the whole of it, simultaneously, like science, we may also see the body as a sort of object, a substance for research. It is my belief that, in doing this, we paradoxically keep our own bodies foreign to us, an unchartered territory.

Ever since Sigmund Freud (1856–1939), we have learned to speak about the "subconscious." The way in which Freud talks about the subconscious is quite materialistic, as if our awareness is a large desk with all kinds of drawers. The bottom drawers of this desk, drawers we can hardly reach, are locked and carry a "No Entry" sign: this is our subconscious. Thinking like this makes human consciousness seem concrete and spatial. You might ask, of course, just where I think the subconscious is and what exactly it is. In answer, I would say that it's a form of awareness, but one still unaware of what might come to awareness.

Some have said that the subconscious *is* the body—a statement that at first glance may seem remarkable. But, think for a moment about how many psychosomatic illnesses there are. The term "psychosomatic" encompasses everything that takes place within our psyche, that we, psychologically speaking, have not assimilated in a proper fashion, and which in one way or another lodge in our body. It is these tensions, accumulating over many years and housed in our body, that make it much harder to assume the proper posture during meditation. Every tension we have not dealt with we encounter in our body through our posture. These tensions make us aware of those issues living within us that we have not come to terms with. We use the Freudian expressions "subconscious" or "unconscious" because we are no longer able reach them. As we try to assume a better, purer posture within meditation, we meet these tensions head on. In this way, the body is something foreign, something objectified, and also a dimension where you either *are* truly yourself or you are invited to *become* truly yourself.

One thing is certain. We in the West—estranged from our bodies because of our culture—have a genuine need to go the way of the body, even if only because the body is something we all have in common with each other, although we are all the masters of our own flesh.

Since the body is also an objective reality, we all share certain facts about our bodies. In this way, our bodies are something collective. However, as soon as we begin to meditate and encounter our tensions and issues, our bodies become personal.

Every form of suffering, physical and psychological, is ours and only ours. Even if we to a certain extent recognize other people's pain, the *experience* itself cannot be shared. This often makes us feel helpless when we see someone else suffering, since we can only guess at what that other person is enduring or experiencing. Therefore, the body is something we all have, and yet something that provides us with a very personal and distinctive experience of ourselves. When we start meditating and feel pain in our joints, muscles, or elsewhere, we begin to realize that we have "processed" so little, that there is still so much within our bodies we have not come to terms with.

This is why adopting the right posture in meditation is an invitation to attain harmony with God, to approach God in an attitude of surrender. Gaining an awareness of the body leads to actualization—allowing God to form and model us. The ancient biblical story of Creation is thus dramatically made present. God is modeling our body in the present. And, as we learn how to adopt the posture more completely and handle our bodies much better, that sentence from the Bible becomes truer: The Lord formed Man, God modeled the body of Man.

The Different Stages of the Body
Because bodily awareness has different stages, layers, and levels, it is necessary to point out several things:

1. Places that Touch
When we talk about caressing and touching, we mainly think about the parts of the body that touch. These parts are located where the body rests. But touching also means surrender, a

coming to rest, a letting go of oneself—something that is made explicit in a gesture of tenderness, when we let ourselves reach out to another. When we meditate correctly, and our body rests upon the earth, we surrender ourselves and let ourselves go. In a profound way, we come to rest. We need to feel how our buttocks and the lower part of our legs touch the ground, and experience this contact as a release, an entrusting ourselves to the earth. Just as we would do when we gesture tenderly to another person, we need to reach out to the earth and become one with it.

2. Inner Space

All meditation postures are good for us because they help us gain an awareness of our inner, physical spaces. This is especially true of the lotus position, which brings attention to our pelvic area. When we adopt this and other positions, the pelvis becomes an open bowl—a shape that makes physical a metaphorical relationship of dependence upon God. An open bowl signifies a receptivity and openness in which all the vital forces located within us achieve awareness. When I adopt the lotus position, I no longer push these forces aside; I no longer become afraid of them. Instead, I feel them unfolding within me, as they make contact with the originator of those senses. I become aware of who I am. I gain confidence and courage by knowing that, such as I am, I come from God's hand. As it says in the Bible: "Another angel, who had a golden censer came and stood at the altar...with the prayers of the saints, the smoke of the incense rose before God from the hand of the angel." (Rev. 8:3–4)

A censer is a bowl filled with incense. When we apply this image of censers full of incense to our becoming a bowl, we become the vessel and the essence that ascends to God. Whatever the nature of those vital forces present in our lives, they are, through our meditation, sacrificed, surrendered, and entrusted to that innermost source.

3. Bone-consciousness

In order for us to sit in the correct posture, it's important not to lean on our muscles (we would soon tire and feel tense if we did). Instead, we have to lean on our *bones*, and, more specifically, our hipjoints—or *ischia*. It's also extremely important that we become aware of the sacrum, or "sacred bone," the last bone of the spine.

In the Bible, the term *flesh* is often paired with the word *bone*. This occurs, for example, in the famous text in which Adam, the Man, recognizes the Woman: "And the Man said, 'This one at last is bone of my bones and flesh of my flesh! She is to be called Woman, because she was taken from Man." (Gen. 2:23) Flesh and bones are paralleled in the following formula of recognition: "All the tribes of Israel then came to David at Hebron, and said, 'Look, we are your own flesh and bone.' " (2 Sam. 5:1)

As we can see, these citations show that combining the words *flesh* and *bone* constitutes a distinct form of belonging, a formula of recognition. Man recognizes Woman as his own, as someone familiar to him. Even though "flesh and bones" is a particular idiom in Hebrew, there is something fundamental being addressed here. Likewise, in the Book of Psalms, you frequently come across the Hebrew word *bone*, which is, as a rule, translated as "vigor." The word *bone* in these contexts possesses something very particular—pointing to something profoundly innate in us. "A kindly glance gives joy to the heart, good news lends strength to the bones," says Proverbs 15.30. Here the word "bones" is synonymous with *heart*—our awareness of our bones thus links us with a very deep self-awareness.

* * *

When we meditate correctly, the phrase "God formed Man from the heart" reveals itself, containing an immense richness that finds expression in our meditation posture. The phrase expresses our physical consciousness, how we become aware of our origin, our surrender to God. In Zazen, this awareness is continued: What took place in the Beginning occurs continually in the present.

❧

3. Breath and Meditation

"GOD BREATHED INTO MAN THE BREATH OF LIFE, and Man became a living being." (Gen. 2:7) This is the fundamental text about human breath. This sentence isn't about a particular time in ancient history, but tells us about how things really are today, about what happens when we breathe. It is *God* who is breathing, yet in such a way that I—a limited, finite being—receive life. In this way, breathing establishes a relationship between us and God, between the finite and the Infinite.

Usually we don't consciously experience our breath, because our conscious self doesn't control it. While we can *will* our arms and legs to move through what physiologists call the central nervous system, our breath (like our heart and digestive system) is governed by the autonomous nervous system. Ordering our heart how to beat or telling our lungs how to breathe has little or no effect on their function.

Yet there does exist a connection between our emotions and these organs—and we can exert an influence on these organs through our consciousness, even if we can't order them around or manipulate them. When it comes to breath, we need to become aware of it, follow it, and sense it. While we cannot hear our breath, we can still listen to it and observe it with our inner self. To do this we need to cultivate both extreme patience and subtle attention. Bu if we do both, we can join our breath and awareness together.

Languages provide us with an important insight here. In Germanic languages, the term *spirit* has nothing whatsoever to do with breath—indeed, the term addresses the intellectual sphere. In Ancient Hebrew, Greek, Latin, and the Romance languages, however, there is a direct association between *spirit* and *breath*. In these languages the term *spirit* signifies first and foremost breath and wind, a stirring of the air, while traces of meaning associated with awareness come second. The associations between breath and spirit are not mere wordplay: they really *do* exist, and, as I will point out, correspond with reality. They indicate that breath and awareness can be linked together, not through the intellect but through the practicing of breathing properly.

Breathing properly and consciously assumes an attitude of openness and attentiveness. Our breath has a connection with the deeper emotional layers of our consciousness. This is evident, for example, when we are very emotional, angry, or anxious. Without our effort, our breathing changes. At the same time, however, our breath remains open to those dimensions of our consciousness where we unfold and become receptive to God. Breathing consciously is hard, because it means not interfering with our breath. We need to discipline ourselves to attain an inner stillness and receptive attention toward God, the God who is our beginning.

While our mind is always looking for fixed and stable forms, breathing is essentially *movement*. Conscious breathing requires us to entrust ourselves to the movement. That's the reason why Jesus combines rebirth and breath in his conversation with Nicodemus (John 3). Nicodemus was a pious, scholarly, and well-respected person. Yet, Jesus told him that as a human being he didn't exist because he was still missing his personal, essential component. It would be the spirit—or rather the breath—that would make Nicodemus familiar with this new life Jesus was offering. It would be a rebirth. Like Nicodemus, we can't bring it about by ourselves, no individual effort will do it; indeed, it is as much as we can do to understand it. We can only allow it to happen to us. Allowing it to happen is being born.

The questions of where our breath comes from and where it goes remain God's secret. God's breath, breathing in us, is the prime author of our rebirth. When we are reborn, our consciousness is set free from its bondage to the ego, because it moves as one with the greater breathing within us. I have a feeling that when we neglect this aspect of breathing in the word of Jesus, His word very much escapes us. This is also true of the words of Jesus in which He speaks of worshiping in truth and spirit. Doesn't this passage signify that our breath has become an act of devotion to Him who is our beginning, and that we too may experience the genuine reality of our existence in this disclosure towards God? (John 4:23)

If we breathe with this awareness, breathing may become a tremendous joy. "Let everything that breathes praise the Lord," declares Psalm 150 with great exuberance. Similarly, breathing links us with all creatures: "Because God's breath fills the entire Earth." (Sirach 1:7). In this way, we feel through our breath the joy of existence.

❦

4. God Sits Enthroned: The Deeper Meaning of Being Seated

MEDITATION IN ACCORDANCE WITH THE method of Zen is primarily a method of being seated. You sit in order to meditate, and being seated is, as it were, a source or method of meditation. East Asia has developed sitting as a technique, as a way of emptying, and as a path to inwardness. The Bible talks about being seated a lot—about God being seated or enthroned in a very special manner—using a symbolic, mythological language. Like most images, the image of being seated is taken from human reality, namely that of the enthronement of an earthly king.

In the Book of Samuel, we read: "Saul was at Gibeah, seated under the tamarisk on the high place, spear in hand, with all his servants standing round him." (1 Sam. 22:6) The detail of sitting is only a coincidental feature in this story, since it mainly deals with the message Saul receives. Nonetheless, we can clearly envisage the scene before us—Saul sitting under a tamarisk, with his spear in his hand, and his courtiers standing to his right and left. The king is sitting and his courtiers are standing.

Likewise, in the First Book of Kings, in which the prophet Micaiah proclaims a vision when he is being consulted by King Achab, Micaiah replies to the king: "Now listen to the word of the Lord. I saw the Lord seated on His throne with the whole array of Heaven standing by Him, on His right hand and on His left." (1 Kings 22:19) Clearly, this representation of an earthly king corresponds with the image of the heavenly king: for the idea of God imagined by the people was that of a king who sat on his throne. So being seated is obviously something royal and somewhat divine, and to us it shows that in some way something must have emanated from the fact of being seated—even if, at the very same time, no one would have had any knowledge whatsoever of what sitting means as it has been developed in Zazen. Nevertheless, the Ancient Hebrews perceived a certain energy in being seated, something that acquired a royal and divine meaning. The question is: Why?

Being Seated

Being seated implies quietness—but quietness altogether different from lying down. When we lie down, we lose attentiveness and are apt to fall asleep. Being seated is, however, an erect posture. However, only if we are sitting properly—and the word *properly* here implies thoughtfulness—does being seated unite in its own special way a sense of tranquility and attentiveness. Being seated is being present in a wakeful and alert rest.

Now, you may be saying to yourself: "Well, I'm not God, therefore enthroning is something that belongs to God not me."

There is, indeed, a difference between our being seated and God being enthroned. For instance, in Psalm 103 it says: "The Lord has fixed His throne in Heaven, His sovereign power rules over all." (103:19) When we sit down, in contrast, we are told to sit firmly on the ground and feel contact with the earth. What this means is that we are being told to be perceptive; we have to become aware of our vulnerability and openness in our contact with the earth. Sitting doesn't come naturally to us. On the contrary it is a painful process of learning. We experience a tremendous amount of tension within us and feel that sense of self-preservation resisting our being seated. And that is why, in our case, we sit on the earth, while God, the origin of all that we are, is enthroned in Heaven.

The last book of the Bible, the Book of Revelation, also refers to the idea of God being enthroned:

> With that, I fell into ecstasy and I saw a throne standing in Heaven, and the One who was sitting on the throne, and the One sitting there looked like a diamond and a ruby. There was a rainbow encircling the throne, and this looked like an emerald. (Rev. 4:2–3).

Here, being seated is actually something heavenly, something divine. A splendor emanates from it. This passage also reveals that God has revealed His kingship to us and has made kings of us, too. We too are called to join in His kingship: "[He] made them a line of kings and priests." (Rev. 5:10) We are called to have a share in it, even if it holds true that we only may receive it, since it is not ours by nature. That is why we may apply these texts about God being seated on His throne to ourselves, because these words were also spoken for us.

Just think about the following declaration Jesus made to His disciples: "I confer a kingdom on you, just as my Father conferred one on me: you will eat and drink at my table in my kingdom, and you will sit on thrones." (Luke 22:29–30) And the passage about the twenty-four elders: "Round the throne in a circle were twenty-four thrones, and on them twenty-four elders sitting." (Rev. 4:4) And in Psalm 113 it says: "He raises the poor from the dust, He lifts the needy from the dunghill, to give them a place among princes, among princes of His people." (Psalms 113: 7–8)

It should be obvious by now that we are also called to be seated and enthroned, to give shape to the regal and divine within us. And that suggests, in a profound manner, the purpose of being seated in meditation; because it is precisely through sitting that this regal and divine quality may lighten up within us. We are created after God's image, and when we are seated this image of God is being realized within us. God's lordship and our call to kingship are not rival interests. God calls us so that in the true and deepest sense of the word we may be *ourselves* and live out the innermost divine core within us. That, in the truest sense, is what it means by being a king.

Enthroned above the Flood

When we look at several passages in the Book of Psalms that talk about being seated or enthroned, it is striking that they always take the shape of a contrast. For instance, in Psalm 29 it says: "The Lord was enthroned for the flood, the Lord sits enthroned as king forever." (Psalm 29:10) In this verse, God sits enthroned above the flood—something that indicates chaos, as we know from the very beginning of the Bible:

> In the beginning God created Heaven and Earth. Now the Earth was a formless void, there was darkness over the deep, with a divine wind sweeping over the waters. (Gen. 1:1–2)

What is important to note here is that that chaos is still present, for at unexpected moments we suddenly encounter what I call the destructive forces present in creation, such as earthquakes, floods, and the like. Yet, in spite of the threat that may emanate from such a chaos, "The Lord was enthroned for the flood."

In a similar way, Psalm 93 offers an even more striking contrast:

> The Lord is king, robed in majesty, robed is the Lord and girded with power. The world is indeed set firm, it can never be shaken; your throne is set firm from of old, from all eternity you exist. (Psalm 93:1–2)

Likewise the passage, "The rivers lift up, O Lord, the rivers lift up their voices, the rivers lift up their thunder"—an image of chaos, of the primal flood—is immediately followed by: "Greater than the voice of many waters, more majestic than the breakers of the sea, the Lord is majestic in the heights." (Psalm 93:3–4) The second passage implies that the force that emanates from the Throne will eventually fracture the destructive force of chaos.

What is being said here about chaos is relevant to the destructive forces we may experience within ourselves as well. Let me explain as follows.

In Zen Buddhism, we often talk of emptiness. In meditation we need to attain emptiness. But the emptiness in meditation does not imply chaos. Rather, it pertains to what Buddhism calls *Nirvana*, or *sunyatta* (as in Mahayana Buddhism): pure being itself. Chaos, on the other hand, in a certain sense corresponds with the Buddhist concept of *samsara*: the primal ocean in which we all float—the ocean of ignorance, desire, and suffering. *Samsara* is a characteristic of human existence. We are adrift in our ignorance, desire, and suffering, until we come to rest in the genuine emptiness of our inner being, that pure essence through which we are freed from this ocean and find, within ourselves, the indestructible vastness of God's enthronement.

When we sit down in meditation, many things start to emerge. We begin to notice the chaos present within us and in our subconscious. In our subconscious, we experience the full extent of our emotions, those powerful forces of desire and emotion that are trying to tear us down and block our inward growth toward the repose of being seated, the stillness of being enthroned.

This is exactly why the image of the Lord who sits enthroned above the flood is such a wonderful icon for meditation. We are sitting, but at the same time our calm of being seated is threatened by everything that goes on within us: our thoughts, imagination, fantasies, and desires. In this way, we need to establish inside ourselves a state of being enthroned above the flood. While we might decide to flee from confronting the chaos and try and cut ourselves off from it, this usually results in stilting our growth.

However, when we dare to risk the confrontation, take the courage to experience all those disorderly forces within us, we grow further into harmony and—better still—integrate those powerful forces within us.

The image of chaos returns repeatedly in the Bible. "God is both refuge and strength for us, a help always ready in trouble," says Psalm 46. "So we shall not be afraid though the Earth be in turmoil, though mountains tumble into the depths of the sea, and its waters roar and seethe, and the mountains totter as it heaves." (Ps. 46:1–3) Again, we encounter the picture of chaos, expressed through natural disasters. This vision of natural destruction is linked with another image of destruction—that of hostile forces threatening Jerusalem, the city of God: "There is a river whose streams bring joy to God's city, it sanctifies the dwelling of the Most High." (v. 4)

Water, and this is true of all the elements, has always had both a positive and negative meaning, destructive as well as constructive. Water is the source of life. A drink of water on a hot day provides wonderful refreshment; it is a symbol of vitality. But water may also destroy. Most of us will, at one time or another, have seen flooded land, and to my mind nothing appears so desolate. Water pulls everything along and, in that sense, is the symbol of the dragging forces of desire and emotions. When you nourish the emotional forces with violence, you become rigid, inflexible, and stiff. But when you accept them without joining them, you mix in the positive life forces. That is why, in meditation, you need to take courage and confront all these forces surging through the subconscious, until the process of integration and purification has taken place.

To do this, often requires a lot of daring and courage. But as portrayed in Chapter Four of the Book of Revelation, when that chaos reappears, the primeval sea has become completely transparent, wholly purified: "In front of the throne was a sea as transparent as crystal." (v.6) This shows that the Book of Revelation is the book of completion.

When we learn to understand what these texts are really trying to tell us about the process of spiritual development, we notice how extraordinarily rich they are in meaning. We can skim the surface of it while we read, but when we learn to recognize the profound meanings, we learn an awful lot about the development we ourselves might experience.

Enthroned above the Peoples

There is still a second contrast, a second antithesis, regarding enthronement: "The Lord is king, the peoples tremble; He is enthroned on the winged creatures, the Earth shivers." (Ps. 99:1–2) "God reigns over the nations, seated on His holy throne....[He] is exalted on high." (Ps. 47:8, 9b)

Historically, these citations refer to a time in which Israel, a superpower at the time of David and Solomon, was receiving tribute from a number of very reluctant serf nations. These nations eagerly awaited the moment when they would regain their independence and were subsequently making aggressive noises. Hostile powers were marching against Israel's rule, which, according to the Bible, is also God's sovereign kingdom. However, as the quotations point out, God sits enthroned over the nations, above the hostile attacks.

In a similar way, most of us fall prey to all sorts of inward aggression, at which moment it's extremely important that we're able to keep our inner calm and quietness. When I am seated in meditation, for example, I notice that I begin to think about all sorts of people who bear a grudge against me, are angry with me, or with whom I have quarreled. All this comes up when we are seated in meditation, and we have to come to terms with it. The question is how?! It's certainly not by encountering these feelings aggressively. Instead, we need to discover in our innermost being the enthronement of God, that peacefulness by which we can transcend aggression and through which we can entrust ourselves to a more profound sense of being.

In the Bible, chaos and the aggression of nations are often perceived as running parallel. In Isaiah 17 is the following beautiful cry:

Disaster! The thunder of vast hordes, a thunder like the thunder of the seas, the roar of nations roaring like the roar of mighty floods, of nations roaring like the roar of the ocean! He rebukes them and far away they flee, driven like chaff on the mountains before the wind, like an eddy of dust before the storm. At evening all is terror, by morning all have disappeared. (vs.12–14)

Isaiah lived in a later era from the Psalmist, when Jerusalem was only a tiny city-state. In Isaiah's time, nothing was left of Israel's worldly powers except for Judea, with Jerusalem as its center, often falling prey to the assaults of the superpowers Assyria and Egypt. What mattered in this precarious situation was the fact that, irrespective of the situation, the Israelites had to rely upon their faith in God enthroned above the nations. They had to maintain that faith and hold on to it, even though at that time it was much harder to believe than in the days when Israel was a political power. In this difficult situation the Israelites had to uphold their faith in the force that eventually would emanate from the calm of God's enthronement, a force that would overcome the aggression approaching them.

This is precisely the point that matters. We all feel threatened when aggression approaches us, because aggression is always destructive. Yet, at these moments, we need to find the calm of being enthroned, of God being enthroned. When we do this, we encounter a force of an entirely different order. It is one attained not by countering aggression with aggression, but one that ultimately allows us to overcome aggression. When we pay close attention to the Bible, in order to understand this force, we find that even in ancient times, God told His people the exact method of dealing with aggression.

The Bible often mentions the battles the Israelites had to fight. On the one hand, these stories might lead us to the impression that these were merely unsavory tribal quarrels that hardly offer an elevating moral. Yet, on the other hand, to the Israelites, these struggles always embodied the very question of their continued existence: Will we be able to stand our ground or will we be destroyed? And, strictly speaking, this situation still holds for us when we are confronted with aggression.

The method the Israelites learned from God was very simple: observe and do not interfere. God told them to face danger whenever necessary; not to hide their heads in the sand, flee, or allow themselves to be defined by fear. He instructed them to encounter danger without interfering and with infinite confidence. Over and over again, we read of how the Israelites possessed so strong a faith that it caused the enemy to flee in panic.

What God in essence said was that the Israelites should observe but not intervene in the aggression, because it was not their concern to force victory—the force of victory resided in God being enthroned. Likewise, being seated in meditation is not a purely passive activity but rather an unfolding to the real, physical power of being. When we face aggression, we become aware of whether that force is truly present. This returns us briefly to Chapter Four of the Book of Revelation: "Flashes of lightning were coming from the throne, and the sound of peals of thunder." (Rev. 4:5) Once we recognize the source, we will experience the power. But the force will only be released through faith.

Enthroned above all Images

Now let's address the third antithesis in the following texts:

> Shame on all who serve images, who pride themselves on their idols; bow down to Him, all you gods! Zion hears and is glad, the daughters of Judah exult, because of your judgments, O God. For you are the Lord, Most High over all the Earth, far transcending all gods. (Ps. 97:7–9)

> Great is the Lord, worthy of all praise, more awesome than any of the gods. All the gods of the nations are idols! (Ps. 96:4–5)

These passages could also be expressed as follows: God sits enthroned above the images, because He sits enthroned above the flood; He sits enthroned above the peoples, and therefore He sits also enthroned above the images.

Now, reading this, you might counter that all our desires and aggressions are accompanied by images, because our emotional forces express themselves through certain images. But what is fundamental in these texts is what is meant by images. In ancient Israel it was forbidden to create images of God. You were not allowed to worship God in the form of a statue.

The purpose for this was as follows: In the nations around Israel, the idea of one God had splintered into many gods—one for every condition of life and a different one for every emergency. These gods found their expression in the form of statues. (It should at this point be stressed that there have always been peoples—particularly in Greece, but also in East and South Asia —who perceived the Infinite beyond statues. In ancient China, Lao Tzu beautifully expressed this as *Tao*—the expression for the Absolute or Infinite. The same can be found in Hinduism and in the Buddhist concepts of *Nirvana* and *sunyatta*, which embody the Infinite or boundless. In Greece, Plato searched for the One, the formless, the Infinite.)

What distinguished the Israelites was that they discovered in God Himself, the Lord of the Covenant, a dimension of the Infinite with whom one could have a personal relationship. Therefore, it was forbidden to make a representation or image of God, because the Israelites knew that the sense of Infinity, the Absolute, and the formless would be splintered and distorted if it was made into an image.

This perception of a new awareness emerges forcefully in the work of Deutero-Isaiah, a contemporary of Lao Tzu and the Buddha. Because of these great minds, human beings were able to progress further toward a new awareness. In Deutero-Isaiah, we can feel the tremendous joy with which this new perception vibrates throughout the author's work, embracing the whole cosmos (plants and animals too are invited to join in this resounding joy). Deutero-Isaiah seeks to proclaim this knowledge to the people and all nations; everyone, says the author, needs to understand that worshiping images is out of date and that identifying the divine with images is something to be ashamed of. This new perception of God is destined to become the center of a new humanity.

When we apply Deutero-Isaiah's revelation to ourselves, I think we'll find that the inclination to create images, in one way or another, is present within each and everyone of us. We all have the tendency to fence in the spiritual and limit the religious experience; we all hedge our conception of God with some sort of idealized image, idea, or system—some representation. The temptation to do this stays with us the entire length of our spiritual journey. Sometimes, it seems as if we freeze the experiences we've had (which are authentic in themselves) and create images of them. As a result, the openness and infinitude are gone.

The knowledge that God sits enthroned above the images carries a very profound energy—for it conceals a deep purpose, which emerges when we begin to express it positively. At that moment, it becomes apparent that God's enthronement is always expressed in the form of, "In His presence are splendor and majesty, in His sanctuary power and beauty." (Ps. 96:6) These are the expressions we continuously come across in this context. I would like to quote here the vision of the prophet Isaiah:

> In the year of King Uzziah's death I saw the Lord seated on a high and lofty throne; His train filled the sanctuary. Above him stood seraphim, each one with six wings: two to cover its face, two to cover its feet, and two for flying; and they were shouting these words to each other: Holy, holy, holy is the Lord of Hosts. His glory fills the whole Earth. (Isa. 6:1–3)

We still sing the refrain during the celebration of every Eucharist: "Holy, holy, holy," after which we declare: "Heaven and Earth are full of His Glory, and full of His Majesty."

What we're celebrating you might say is the splendor of being that is present everywhere, a glory we normally cannot see because our vision isn't pure enough. Sometimes, at a favorable moment, we suddenly perceive how luminous everything is. This can happen to us while we're walking in nature. Suddenly, we experience this brightness of being, the radiance of Heaven and Earth. But, at the very moment we experience it, we rigidly begin to categorize the mental images that arise in our consciousness, and our vision is once more confined and we no longer perceive that luminescence of everything around us. God is present in that brightness of being—but only on condition that we transcend all images, all those boundaries that limit and splinter the conception of God. This destructive force has manifested itself in the religious wars and ecclesiastical quarrels that have marked the last three millennia.

This is also the challenge that comes from the process of meditation, "being enthroned above the images." Being seated becomes of great importance, in the sense that being seated becomes an existential experience. It's important to emphasize that that existential experience doesn't exclude formal religious convictions; but those convictions cannot be anything else than the result of what has been brought to light by a profound experience of oneness. These experiences of oneness must be the soul and inspiration of all that is intellectually formed.

As you can see, there is great wealth hidden in the biblical expression "the enthronement of God." The feeling of that enthronement—above the flood of desires, above false, deeply entrenched images—must all be experienced, in its entirety, while we're seated! We are, as it were, invited to rehearse the event by which God is enthroned and make it, in its truest sense, our reality.

Sitting is Beholding

There is still one more aspect about sitting that needs to be mentioned: That being seated is not only about being, it is also about perceiving. This is perhaps the subtlest and most complex feature of God's enthronement. Consider the following passage:

> The Lord is in His holy temple! The Lord, His throne is in Heaven; His eyes watch over the world, His gaze scrutinizes the children of Adam. The Lord examines the upright and the wicked, the lover of violence He detests. (Ps. 11:4–5)

God *perceives*, a feature that is also noted of earthly kings: "A king who sits on his throne of judgment winnows all evil with his eyes." (Eccl. 20:8) In this passage, the writer observes that the king, sitting on his seat of judgment, emanates a force; with a penetrating eye, the king winnows evil.

I am fully aware that this is a delicate issue to elucidate, since what God *sees* has often been used to frighten people, to such an extent that (which is worse) the whole conception of God becomes affected by fear. We're all familiar with sayings that God sees everything; as if God were a kind of cane, conveniently concealed behind the door, with which we can be chastened. Thus, if, from the outset, God becomes a source of anxiety for us, we often need a substantial process of purification to come to terms with the anxiety.

Yet, when the Bible talks about God seeing, the intent is not to frighten, although fear may come in once in a while. For example, in Job, it says: "Since his days are measured out, since his tale of months depends on you…turn your eyes from him, leave him alone." (Job 14:5–6a) Then the passage continues: "Like a hired laborer, to finish his day in peace." (v.6b) What this statement sounds like is a human being saying: "God, could you keep your distance and close your eyes for a minute so I can enjoy my life?" This very human desire is one of many throughout the Bible, which, after all, is meant to be a book where we human beings can recognize ourselves.

In Psalm 7 we read:

Lift Thyself up against the fury of my enemies: from Thee proceeds justice and the council of gods surrounds Thee:

and over it take Thy seat on high. Lord, Thou who art judge of peoples, grant me justice O Lord, according to my righteousness, and according the integrity that is in me. Do you not try hearts and minds, O God, who is a righteous judge? (vs.7–9b, 10)

These kinds of passages originate from the Israelite administration of justice. For the benefit of people who stood accused and knew themselves to be innocent, the Israelites thought a kind of Divine Judgment existed in which God had to determine who was ultimately guilty and who was not. Thus the worshipper put himself into God's care, in order that God would reveal his innocence; because God could fathom the depth of the accused's heart and marrow. God could probe and look right through us.

Thus, for the individual totally convinced of his innocence and honesty, the only option was to commit himself wholly unto God, so that God would publicly and plainly establish his innocence. In this situation, the all-seeing eye of God becomes not condemnatory but salvific. Because God sees me, He will not condemn me as people do. God *knows* I am innocent. When people judge me with their minds, their judgment petrifies me, arouses feelings of guilt and inferiority in me. Being seen by God, however, is totally different. It calls forth the very best in me. While my shortcomings are not glossed over, they are regarded as part of the entire process through which I am trying to bring out the best in myself. By affirming this knowledge, I can outgrow the faults and shortcomings I have.

Nothing, therefore, is more disastrous for the child when he or she is told, even lightheartedly, that, if they do anything wrong

God is watching. The child is inhibited from gaining self-reliance, from growing into him- or herself, and from having a self-confident faith in God. And this, surely, is the whole point—to gain from self-confidence a trust in our own integrity and innocence, under the eye of God, who can see that innocence and can demonstrate it.

A quote from Psalm 33 is apposite here:

> From Heaven the Lord looks down, He sees all the children of Adam, from the place where He sits He watches all who dwell on the Earth; He alone molds their hearts, He understands all they do. (vs.13–15)

Here, the vision of God is expressed almost triumphantly, with joy. Likewise, in the following beautiful and truly profound vision of God (no mention of being enthroned here) from Psalm 139:

> O Lord, you examine me and know me, you know when I sit, when I rise, you understand my thoughts from afar. You watch when I walk or lie down, you know every detail of my conduct. You created my inmost self, knit me together in my mother's womb. For so many marvels I thank you; a wonder am I, and all your works are wonders. You knew me through and through, my being held no secrets from you, when I was being formed in secret, textured in the depths of the Earth. Your eyes could see my embryo. In your book all my days were inscribed, every one that was fixed is there. How hard for

me to grasp your thoughts, how many, God, there are!
(Ps. 139:1–3, 13–17)

The passage above offers a real commitment to God's omniscience and all-encompassing vision. As Meister Eckhart has so beautifully stated: The eye with which we see God is the same eye with which God perceives us. We can turn it around, and say that the eye with which God beholds us is the same eye with which we behold God. Being seated provides a very special form of self-awareness by which our body gains sight. When I am seated, my pelvis, sacrum, and spinal cord attain vision; the deep neediness within me lights up as a desire for perception, and my buried aggressive feelings experience light. In equal measure, my self-assured vision of seeing and being seen by God becomes purer and more balanced and an openness grows into what the Japanese call *kensho* and the Germans *wesenschau*—the contemplative vision of clear, pure being.

The Flemish mystic Jan van Ruysbroek articulated it as follows: "What we are, we gaze upon, and what we gaze upon, we are." To behold what one is, and to be what one beholds, is the key formula of illumination. We see what we are and are what we see. This is also the innermost meaning of what the Bible is saying about being seated. Being seated is perceiving. God in Heaven is seated on high, His eyes searching and perceiving. Accordingly, as we reach that brightness of vision in meditation, this word applies to us, too. In our being seated lies concealed an enormous wealth; and as we evolve in our practice, the enthronement of God is consummated within us. So, the Bible is here a kind of manual. Although it doesn't furnish us with a method for being seated, it does point out the entire road of development. God is seated above the flood. He sits enthroned above the images. Sitting is being and being seated is perceiving.

5. The Underworld in Our Heart

IN THE BOOK OF PROVERBS WE FIND THE
following lines: "Death and the underworld lie open before
the Lord. How much more the heart of the children of men!"
(15:11)

This quotation is a declaration about God's omniscience—
albeit a rather formal and theological one. However, when
something is said about God, something is also being asserted
about us. We're being told something about us, in the form of a
process, about something we need to experience. I think this
process takes place in meditation, especially in Zen meditation.

Let's look at the quotation. It is striking that the passage
makes a comparison between "death and the underworld" and the
"hearts of the children of men." It is noticeable that, although
"death and the underworld" are those places that are remotest
from God, God is nevertheless still present. In itself, the underworld implies the chaotic—that which acts against life, light, and
the transparency of God. The passage is drawing a correlation
between "death and the underworld" on one hand and "the hearts

of the children of men" on the other; and that correlation lies in that both are open to God.

As I mentioned in Chapter Three, we have only been learning to talk about the subconscious for a century. As I also pointed out, we conceive of the subconscious in a material way, as a kind of house and cupboard. As I suggested, I think we think *too* materially about the subconscious; even though I cannot deny that from ancient times we have thought of the many hiding places that lurk within our consciousness and heart in visual terms—those imponderable, inaccessible places that somehow play a part in who we are but of which we are either barely aware or completely ignorant.

However we visualize our subconscious, we certainly identify ourselves with particular aspects of our consciousness—usually also in terms of angles or experiences that lie within us, such as touch, joy, or comfort—although we also ignore or don't know about other aspects of our consciousness that also exercise their influence upon us. If I were asked to define or localize the subconscious, I would say that the subconscious *is* the body. It's perhaps an exaggeration to say so, but there is some truth to it: For everything we experience—physically or psychically—in one way or another deposits a sediment in our body and stockpiles it. These experiences amass themselves in the recesses, the parts of ourselves we're unaware of or are aren't revitalized by our living energies. So, to all intents and purposes, the subconscious *is* the body.

It should be obvious to readers by now that, through posture and breathing, the body plays a major role in Zen meditation. Body-posture and breathing are, as it were, the material needed to begin Zen meditation—material we cannot escape from. As I've said many times, meditation leads us to join with being, to come to terms with the essence of life. But such ringing promises of liberation and openness cannot disguise the fact that there is a considerable amount of struggle, wrestling, and suffering that takes place on the journey. The journey involves confronting our darker shadow, that antagonistic side that we want to close our eyes to but from which we cannot escape, because we're bound up by our physicality and our breath. We collide against that other side, as if it were a wall. This is a process of purification.

In the Book of Proverbs, we regularly come across the declaration, "God tries the heart of men." (Prov. 16:2) This statement refers also to the process of being tried by purification—one perhaps clarified by another passage: "A furnace for silver, a foundry for gold, but God for the testing of hearts!" (Prov. 17:3) The purification involves our experiencing a refinement of our selves to the essential core. In general, we tend to see things in specific patterns that keep turning up in our mind, and render particular ways of doing and thinking absolute. When we are refined, however, we begin to see things in relative terms.

We've all heard the recurrent old songs in our head. We've all experienced our self-justifications, prejudices, and specious thinking in trying to project a certain self-image. In the stillness of meditation, all these facets of our unexamined selves emerge in our consciousness. At the same time, when we try and deal with these recurrent themes, our stillness disappears. What has happened is that we've moved away from our inner essence and are inhabiting an area of self-preservation. While, of course, this more engaged level of consciousness is important for us, since it's the place where we develop our abilities and live an active life, it is not where we need to be in meditation. In meditation, we're taken from that place and drawn back into the depths, which is both the underworld of our internal chaos and at the same time, as the quotation that began this chapter suggests, a place where God is present and beginning to shine forth.

This is the place the mystics talk about when they mention "the foundation of the soul." It is a place where our consciousness reaches oneness. This oneness of consciousness is where *all* our abilities and all that is creative reside. It is the source of our unfolding and the source of the being which experiences the unfolding. And it is arrived at when, sitting perfectly quietly, we adopt the right posture.

When we feel our breath calming and are able to relinquish everything and admit anything, this is a sign we are really residing in that fundamental essence of soul, that substance of being. It is then we have been refined through struggle. God tries the hearts. Through that struggle we gain a new way of knowing ourselves and inhabiting our selves. Through that struggle we are able to gaze with equanimity upon all those comparatively unwelcome parts of our self.

* * *

Consider the shepherd who sets out with his sheep. He could, should he wish, worry about what happens to every single sheep. Or, he could be present, serene, and give his sheep ample space with which to roam about. As long as he is present, all is fine. The shepherd in the second scenario doesn't try to control everything, but lets it develop as it evolves. He is present, aware; but at the same time he doesn't interrupt the flow.

In this second scenario, we, like the shepherd, experience the root of our being. We start to see through things, understand ourselves fully, and ascertain the transience of everything. We let things happen. There are moments of despair and genuine pain, as we move from asserting ourselves vigorously to surrendering ourselves to the calm and stillness that transcends us. The old "I" never dies without a reason. However, after we have gone through that despair and darkness, there is light, clarity, and purity, and some sort of liberation has taken place. At the same time, we feel that we have drawn much closer to that innermost part of ourselves, have gained a new and incredibly intimate form of self-knowledge, akin to the knowledge of God:

Death and the underworld lie open before the Lord. How much more the hearts of the children of men!

❦

6. The Irradiating Face

Let the light of your face shine on us.
(Psalm 4:6; cp. Num. 6:25)

WHEN I VISITED JAPAN, I WAS STRUCK BY the importance the Japanese seemed to place in sculptures of the Buddha, and the role they played whenever you bowed or prostrated yourself before them. Do these statues really represent an external reality, one we need to focus ourselves on? It certainly appears they do.

The story goes that, when the Buddha was born, he immediately took seven steps in ten directions. While this is surely a legend, the story does say something profound: It emphasizes the awareness of direction and the ability to focus oneself. For Buddhists, the Buddha is considered a living reality in his representations, and in bowing devotees focus on this actuality: For "bowing to" means being "focused on." However, it's important to realize that there is no difference between the inner and the outer. For the very thing that transcends us is reflected within ourselves. People sometimes need an image, icon, a cultic object, altar, or tabernacle to focus their attention on; but these things don't take the place of inner reflection. In Buddhist tradition, it is said that prostrating yourself before an image is necessary in order to protect the monk from the weakness of vanity that might be evoked as a result of concentrating too much on the internal. This sense of *focusing* is something not just particular to Buddhism, or Asian religions in general.

Let's look more deeply at the epigraph to this chapter: "Let the light of your face shine on us." Here we are focused on God's face. The questions remain: Why are we focusing on God's face and from what perspective?

Reflections

When we sit together in meditation, we continually experience a shattering of our consciousness into a thousand—even a hundred thousand—pieces. These pieces reflect back to us the brokenness and fragmentation of our existence and consciousness, and threaten us with disintegration. We all carry within ourselves the potential of final rupture, the ultimate shattering by death.

Yet, at the same time, we are offered oneness through the light of God's countenance. This, as it is depicted in the Psalms, is a struggle of life with death. It is striking that light and perception are often paired as expressions for God's countenance in the Psalms: "the light of your countenance," "seeing the countenance," (Ps. 4:6; 11:7; 16:11; 17:15; 21:7), and "in the light of your countenance restoration." (Ps. 80:4, 8:20)

While these passages are concerned with the experience of oneness ("Let the light of your face shine on us"), there are other moments that are exemplified by passages, such as "standing before His countenance, sitting and walking for His face" (Ps. 56:14; 61:8; 102, 29; 116:9; 140:14), that point to an inner pattern, originating from that countenance. The image that constantly lingers in the background is one we're familiar with: the comparison between the heavenly and earthly king. When the Israelites visited the earthly king, they beheld him; to "encounter" him was to see him. However, the beautiful phrasing of "standing before His countenance" offers a much richer image than the translation we would tend to give it, namely as "looking at" or "someone in the service of" the king.

The act of contemplating His countenance is prepared by the inner pattern that's so important in Zazen. In Zazen we have to return, time and again, to the proper bearing and the appropriate sequence of our breath. When we focus in this manner, we experience oneness. This inner order flourishes by itself—and not just in Zazen, but in daily life. We *live and sit* before God's countenance, experiencing quietness and inner consistency; we *walk* before God's countenance, the representation of the inner patterning of our life's path; we *stand* before God's countenance, representing the compassion and charity that comes from the realization of that oneness.

This experience of oneness is an encounter of life with death, of life *through* death. And from the rupture that death provides, we regain wholeness anew. In the Old Testament, the idea of life through death came about through an awareness of direction, as the Israelites focused on the sanctuary, in which God's face was present, and which was thought to be connected with the Ark (see for example Josh. 6 and Sam. 6). That the Israelites were aware of direction implies that the external symbol, detached from the self, is important. While that is true, it is not everything. For the symbol of God's countenance refers to the fact that God is in *every* direction and, at the same time, His countenance is reflected in my innermost core. With this understanding, we can ask, to paraphrase Psalm 139: "Whither shall I go from Your Breath? Whither shall I flee from Thy countenance? Wherever I go, I shall always feel Thy Breath within me. The life-giving Breath of God is always within me. And wherever I go, I shall always encounter the countenance of God, regardless the direction I choose."

* * *

The countenance of God reflects itself in my innermost being. This is what the great prophets Elijah and Elisha experienced as the cornerstone of their prophetic mission: "God—His Countenance—before whom I stand." (1 Kings 17:1; 18:15) Usually this passage is translated as "in whose service I am," which, while accurate, fails to elucidate the experience of oneness, or of the light from which the prophets lived and worked.

Why does the phrase "Let the light of your face shine on us" resonate so deeply? I suggest it is because so many of us, immersed in the greatest struggle we know—the struggle of life with death— seek guidance from the principle of oneness, the face that lightens. That face is what has brought us from death to life, that saved Elijah and Elisha when they were threatened with destruction, that gave them inner unity and calm and allowed them to rest: "And the diversity, the multitude of time, went from them." Time, which shows the disintegration of our earthly existence, suddenly vanishes because we have attained another dimension. Our physical pain falls away when we find rest in the tranquility of His countenance.

When you leaf through the Bible, you notice how often the term "God's countenance" is talked about and pleaded for. Moses, for instance, implores God: "Let me see your countenance, for the light of your face is the richest gratification." He receives the answer: "But my face you cannot see, for no human being can see me and survive." (Ex. 33:18, 20).

It is because of this, that the light must enter the darkness again to become more light. You can never possess the light as such and never make it your own, except than by striking upon the darkness. But the darkness is lightening itself, because through the darkness itself, we are lifted above the limitation of our consciousness. Darkness cloaks us human beings within the infinite space of God's countenance. The darkness of emptiness is always the gate to the light:

Let the light of your face shine on us.

❦

7. What Is Silence?

THERE ARE SO MANY LEVELS, FORMS, OR ASPECTS of keeping quiet, that it's far from easy to answer the question: "What is silence?" For a start, silence can be a negative as well as a positive thing. For instance, in human relationships, silence may be the inability to express oneself. In spite of how physically close you are to your partner, there might be a massive separation between you emotionally. Sometimes this isolation is filled with hate and bitterness. Then again, silence might also be unhappy self-involvement; or the first, shy experience of meeting another person, which might be a moment of peace, filled with tenderness. Silence might also be a moment of reprieve, of expectancy, of something new that arouses interest in you toward another. Sometimes we are silent in resignation as we succumb to the inevitable. At other times, we are silent in wonder and admiration. Then, finally, there is the tranquility that contains the fullness of a presence. At that point, there is such an overflowing, from one to the other, that nothing can describe the profound oneness that is experienced.

Virtually all of these experiences of silence are present when we reflect on that stillness in relation to the Absolute and where the Presence is clearly distinguished. By way of illustration, let us take the story of Elijah from the Bible (1 Kings 19:1–18).

The story begins with the stillness of loneliness and despair, brought about by Jezebel's threat to kill the prophet. Elijah leaves his servant in a village at the edge of civilization and flees into the desert. He lies down under a broom tree and prays that he may die on the spot. After this prayer, the stillness of sleep descends upon him—something that shows that being aware of our predicaments offers us some rest. Suddenly, something unexpected happens: an angel touches Elijah (he is touched by invisible reality) and he experiences a new aspect of tranquility. You can feel Elijah's amazement when he discovers that the angel has prepared food and drink for him. Then Elijah falls asleep again—a new lull. Again he is touched by the angel and told to undertake a journey to Horeb, the mountain of God, which lies in heart of the desert.

While this voyage is a physical one, it is at the same time an internal excursion, an inner process experienced in complete silence. When Elijah arrives at the mountain of God, he enters a cave and stays there overnight. That cave is, as we might expect, a symbol of withdrawal into one's personal subconscious, into the intimacy of one's being. The withdrawal into the cave signifies a confrontation with the self. As God says to Elijah: "What are you doing here Elijah?" This is the moment when Elijah can tell his story, can verbalize what has befallen and stalled him.

After this confrontation with himself, Elijah is ready for his encounter with God. This dialogue with the Divine comes about through various phases. God tells Elijah to leave the cave. Then

God unleashes destructive forces that are part of our natural cosmos—storm, earthquake, and fires—and which Elijah has to endure. Although these are the traditional signs of the manifestation of the Divine, on this occasion Elijah learns that God is present in none of these destructive powers. The natural disasters' only purpose is to unwind all the straps that keep men dedicated to a cause, to reduce Elijah to utter and sheer loneliness, and throw him into the abyss of his singular existence. Only when this has happened can the wonder of silence come to pass in the rustling of a soft breeze—a still small voice. Here there is a fullness of presence, a deep sense of security.

From that fullness comes the question again: What are you doing here? This renewed confrontation no longer terrifies Elijah. It is but preparation for his mission—that is, acceptance of a new assignment in the tangible reality of human existence, taken from total immersion in the natural world into tranquility. In addition, Elijah learns that, however important his mission might be, it is God Himself who enacts His plan in the history of mankind.

If we reduce any of these aspects, angles, and shades of stillness to two basic elements, we can say that stillness is always a matter of confrontation with the self and with one's darker traits. However, silence may also at the same time be the abundance of God's presence. The story of Elijah is only an example. Thematically, the Bible is not very explicit on the topic of stillness or tranquility, but there is silence throughout the Bible. If you read between the lines, you will find stillness substantially associated with many other themes. Precise clues about stillness are also found in a multitude of ascetic and mystical manuscripts, in Western as well as Asian monastic traditions.

Those who are prepared to enter the path of silence, the path of turning toward one's own heart, will discover how profoundly human this approach is, how truly quintessential a part it is of being human—for all seasons and in all ages.

❧

8. Form Is Emptiness, Emptiness Is Form

AS I HAVE NOTED, IN BUDDHIST MONASTERIES you endlessly hear the recitation and chanting of "form is emptiness, emptiness is form." The first half of the chant tells us how all forms and shapes we perceive are ultimately empty—for, whatever they pretend to be, these forms and shapes are in their deepest essence genuinely *nonexistent* (in the literal sense of the word). That is why every form and shape is, in the end, empty. What is interesting is that Zen Buddhism adds at the same time that emptiness is also form. This is to remind us that, should we think silence is absolute and that we have pierced through form and arrived at emptiness, we are in fact creating a division. To consider only that form is emptiness is to incorrectly divide human existence. This is why Zen Buddhists immediately add to the expression "form is emptiness" the assertion that "emptiness is form."

I want to discuss this chant in the light of the Book of Ecclesiastes. This book does not directly use the term emptiness but instead uses the word "vanity." It's a familiar phrase, almost a slogan, in Ecclesiastes: "Vanity of vanities, all is vanity"—a (Hebrew) way of saying, "the height of vanity." (cp. Song of Songs)

The author (let us call him the Preacher) who speaks these words doesn't assert them in a philosophical, almost hymnal manner such as the monks in the Buddhist practice do. In these texts, the Preacher attempts—in a philosophical sense—to analyze existence, although there is a hymnal quality to the words that makes the emptiness stand out.

The Preacher in Ecclesiastes is like someone who bashes his head against a wall time and again. Because neither life nor wisdom bring what they seem to promise, the Preacher is continually frustrated. He has been raised in the traditional schools of wisdom in which the use, importance, and success of wisdom is constantly recommended. The Preacher has asked what the use or advantage of such knowledge is and has come to the painful realization every time he thinks about it that it is of no use or purpose. Hence the verdict and leitmotif: "Vanity of vanities, all is vanity."

In a certain sense the Preacher's recognition is similar to what we've discovered about Asian concepts of emptiness: "Everything is emptiness." Let's, therefore, analyze the Preacher's words more closely, not philosophically but practically. The Preacher looks at various aspects of existence that, because of innumerable setbacks, lead him to the same conclusion—that all is in vain, or at least not what it seemed to promise.

The Book of Ecclesiastes starts with the figure of Solomon, the apex of wisdom and enjoyment. Whatever way you look at it, Solomon's life story seems exceptionally disappointing. He seemed so wise, so wealthy, and so able to enjoy himself. And yet, in the end, it all meant nothing:

> I have acquired a greater stock of wisdom than anyone before me in Jerusalem. I myself have mastered every kind of wisdom and science. I have applied myself to understanding philosophy and science, stupidity and folly, and I now realize that all this too is chasing after the wind. "Much wisdom, much grief; the more knowledge, the more sorrow." (Eccl. 1:16–18)

It is enjoyable to be wise, but what happens then? The more we understand, the greater our grief or sorrow is. We are profoundly affected by the sorrow that fills human existence and marks our experience. It is an inescapable and intimate fact of our lives.

> More is to be gained from wisdom than from folly, just as one gains more from light than from darkness; this, of course, I see: "The wise have their eyes open, the fool walks in the dark." No doubt! But I know, too, that one fate awaits them both. (Eccl. 2:13–14)

The Preacher can see that it is better to be wise, but also understands the limitations of the benefit of that knowledge. This contravenes the teaching of the traditional schools of wisdom, in which the author of Ecclesiastes was raised, where wisdom was considered something absolute and its tenets unequivocal. While the Preacher recognizes the light of wisdom, to him that light is always limited: "And I said to myself that this also is vanity." So where is the advantage? What is the purpose? "And I said to myself that this also is vanity." (Eccl. 2:15)

After this, the Preacher presents a sort of analysis of existence, in which he draws the conclusion that all phenomena occur simultaneously and paired (reminding us of the Chinese *yin* and *yang*). The Preacher lists a few examples:

> There is a season for everything, a time for every occupation under Heaven: A time for giving birth, a time for dying; a time for planting, a time for uprooting what has been planted. A time for killing, a time for healing; a time for knocking down, a time for building. (Eccl. 3:1–3)

And it continues:

> A time for searching, a time for losing; a time for keeping, a time for discarding....A time for loving, a time for hating; a time for war, a time for peace. (Eccl. 3:6 and 8)

And concludes:

> What do people gain from the efforts they make? I contemplate the task that God gives humanity to labor at. (Eccl. 3:9–10)

Everything that occurs falls ultimately back to God. God is the force that operates in human existence; God is also the origin of existence; everything is reduced to God. In Ecclesiastes, God becomes the unfathomable. Despite the phenomena he has encountered in his existence, and which can't answer his most profound questions, the Preacher discovers that God is not obscured, there is still that reality of God. God, however, has now become the totality of the Preacher's unknowing.

> I contemplate the task that God gives humanity to labor at. All that He does is apt for its time; but although He has given us an awareness of the passage of time, we can grasp neither the beginning nor the end of what God does. (Eccl. 3:10–11)

God has installed something of the Absolute in us. But everything that exists is confined. You are always confronted with limitations; that means one moment everything seems fine, and the next it isn't.

> I know that whatever God does will be forever. To this there is nothing to add, and from this there is nothing to subtract.... (Eccl. 3:4a)

This last assertion originally refers to the law—we're not allowed to add to it or take from it. For the Preacher, this law now applies to human existence; existence can't be changed or improved. Immediately, there follows another statement:

> God has made it so, in order that men should fear him. (Eccl. 3:14b)

Traditionally, in the Bible, the term "fear of God" signifies obedience to God. But the word "fear" implies an emotional factor. It obviously contains a risk! When you don't obey, you're doomed. Obedience is not only a practical affair, but it's also necessary in order to save your life. Still, that isn't all that can be said about fear for, in the Scriptures, obedience to God is based on an appearance of God, a theophany.

God, for instance, can appear in a fire. This is an image that reflects energy. We might think of high voltage cables. When you come into contact with their charge, you may be killed unless you are properly prepared. When it comes to meeting God, preparing yourself properly might take the shape of ritual or duty. In such a way, the overwhelming force of God is channeled down to your level and transformed into a way you can live with. Whenever the Bible uses the phrase "fear of God" for dutifulness, there is, at least in the background, always an idea of emotional direction. The obedience means you have to commit yourself. This is the way in which one attunes oneself to God, who is the source of life.

How does the Preacher manage to experience both the ominous but also life-giving power of God? The answer is through the acknowledgment and experience of emptiness! Because he understands that everything is ephemeral and vain, the Preacher can draw closer to the transcendent, overwhelming force of a God whom he can never manipulate or program. The question now is how this attitude toward life manifests itself in the Preacher's thoughts. Wouldn't he now be so pessimistic or dour that the richness of life didn't express itself at all?

Well, this isn't the case. No one uses the word joy as often as the Preacher does. As well as deep depression and darkness in

Ecclesiastes, you can also find the opposite—joyfulness and gladness.

This is exactly the same as in Buddhism's conclusion that emptiness is form. There is a well-known story in Buddhism in which a pupil asks his Zen master: "What is Zen?", or "What is Enlightenment?" The Zen master replies: "Have you had your breakfast?" "Yes," replies the pupil. Whereupon the master says: "Then wash your breakfast utensils."

Zen is doing what you have to do. Zen is not enlightenment, nor is it a false, pure inwardness, or transcendence. No, Zen is very tangible: do this, do that, and remain open to reality—now. The Preacher reaches a similar conclusion, and in an unexpected, almost hedonistic manner:

> I know there is nothing better for them than to be happy
> and enjoy themselves as long as they live. And also that it
> is God's gift to men that every man should eat and drink
> and take pleasure in all his toil. (Eccl. 3:12–13)

The emptiness is full—and in that way positive. It's not positive in that you can lay your hands on it, but positive in that it is awarded to you at every instant as a gift of God. This shouldn't surprise us, for in the biblical tradition, "eating and drinking" always count as gifts of God. This especially holds true when it is a result of the "word" spoken by God.

When, for example, God presents the law in the desert, it starts to rain. This indicates that it is possible to live from the word of God and His law. This is a profound notion you will find throughout the Bible. Ecclesiastes suggests that, when we finally come to accept emptiness and live with it, emptiness becomes an art of living, even a joy. We learn to enjoy the moment; we eat and drink from it. In the immediacy of the gift we have gratefully received from God, emptiness becomes form and emptiness is form.

Let us accompany the Preacher still further in his odyssey. One of the things profoundly ingrained in the Bible and in Israel's schools of wisdom is the teaching of retribution—if you do only good, then good will also befall you and no harm will come your way. If you do wrong, then things will also go ill with you. Therefore, the Preacher says:

> Yet this too I know [from the schools of wisdom], that there is no good in store for people who fear God, because they fear him [fear equals compliance to God, in the traditional sense: "fear of God"]. But there is no good in store for the wicked because he does not fear God, and so, like a shadow, he will not prolong his days. Another futile thing that happens on Earth; upright people being treated as though they were wicked and wicked people being treated as though they were upright. To me this is one more example of futility. (Eccl. 8:12b–14)

Our deepest notions about retribution don't plumb the depths, because retribution is empty, in vain. The Preacher then continues:

> And therefore I praise joy, since human happiness lies only
> in eating and drinking and in taking pleasure; this comes

from what someone achieves during the days of life that God gives under the sun. (Eccl. 8:15)

Therefore, the Preacher approaches wisdom as something very relative. What he emphasizes is that we should just live in the immediacy of the present and enjoy it. That, to Ecclesiastes, is "illumination":

> Having applied myself to acquiring wisdom and to observing the activity taking place in the world—for day and night our eyes enjoy no rest—I have scrutinized God's whole creation: you cannot get to the bottom of everything taking place under the sun; you may wear yourself out in the search, but you will never find it. Not even a sage can get to the bottom of it, even if he says that he has done so. (Eccl. 8:16–17)

"God's whole creation" is an expression of the Preacher. That "work" is incomprehensible. Everything that happens possesses, in the main, a component of unknowing. Even though the wise men say they know, in fact they don't. That is the Preacher's major criticism of the traditional schools of wisdom, and their attempts to "objectify" wisdom. Therefore, returning briefly to his teaching on retribution, he says:

> Do not be upright to excess and do not make yourself unduly wise: why should you destroy yourself? Do not be wicked to excess, and do not be a fool: why die before your time? It is wise to hold on to one and not let go of

75

the other, since the godfearing will find both. (Eccl. 7:16–18)

By noting that he who fears God clings to both, the Preacher even perceives morality as relative. He advises that we shouldn't expect too much of morality, because morality cannot find a way out for us, can't make life less of a riddle. In the same way, the Preacher says that we shouldn't brush morality aside, since it has its own significance. Thus, we shouldn't act foolishly. The Preacher bridges even the contradiction between what is right and what is wrong—it is unified in what he calls the "fear of God." This awe, this holy reverence, manifests itself in the realization that the work of God is ultimately empty and impenetrable. The Preacher recognizes that here at least wisdom has its advantages:

And the advantage of knowledge is this: that wisdom bestows life on those who possess her. Consider God's creation: who, for instance, can straighten what God has bent? When things are going well, enjoy yourself, and when they are going badly, consider this: God has designed the one no less than the other so that we should take nothing for granted. (Eccl. 7:12b–14)

What the Preacher is saying here is that even though you may feel everything is fine, that you understand and know how to move forward, a bad day will come along, your whole theory will be smashed to smithereens, and you will experience the moment of emptiness again:

This alone is my conclusion: God has created man straightforward, and human artifices are human inventions. (Eccl. 7:29)

What this passage literally says is: "God made men upright, but they sought out many thoughts." Well, here you precisely find the purpose of meditation: to thrust through that multitude of thoughts we experience within ourselves into the simplicity of our essential nature—that state where we came forth from God's hand, naked and pure.

While the Preacher senses something of that original existing simplicity, we can't assign either form or figure to it, because everything is empty. The only way we can experience it is in the present, the actual now: to enjoy that which has been given in the immediacy of the present:

And whenever God gives someone riches and property, with the ability to enjoy them and to find contentment in work, this is a gift from God. (Eccl. 5:18)

Only in connection with the immediacy of the present does the Preacher speak about God in a positive manner, and only then does he suggest the establishment of a positive relationship.

This is ultimately what the Preacher is saying about the teaching of emptiness experienced in daily life. In daily life, we're able to catch a glimpse of God while enjoying and rejoicing in the small things we're given. We can enjoy everything, freely given, but only in the immediacy of the present. For, as soon as we want to take that gift, it's gone, nothing, a zero. But, when we are deeply and sufficiently convinced of the notion of emptiness, then we may enjoy the gift as something beautiful.

This experience of inwardness can never be severed from daily life. In daily life, enlightenment comes about by simply doing what we have to do—without expecting anything or wanting to attain a thing. Enlightenment comes about in doing things that need to be done of their own accord.

❦

9. Earth and Heaven

In the Beginning God created Heaven and Earth. (Gen.1)

IN A MANNER THAT REMINDS US OF THE CHINESE *yin* and *yang*, at the very beginning God divides Himself into Heaven and Earth. Heaven and Earth don't just stand side by side, but are diametrically opposed—just as *yang* is the active and *yin* the passive principle. Other opposites in Chinese cosmology are the mountain and valley, masculine and feminine, giving and receiving. In this way the original unity in the act of creation is rendered into notions of polarity: Heaven and Earth.

To my mind, Heaven and Earth both determine what happens in Zazen. Earth is dust, matter. In Zazen we share in that Earth, through our body, when we place emphasis upon our bodily posture. We become aware that "Earth" is within us, and we give a particular form to that "Earth." Heaven, on the other hand, assumes a whole gamut of meanings: It is the blue firmament above us, and something that transcends us; it is the ultimate that presents itself to us in a luminous void and a paradigm of the focused and undivided attention of Zen, of nonobjective contemplation. In a similar way, the sky is empty, formless, an expression of God's infinitude—of happiness. The quest for an empty, clear, and, therefore, vigorous consciousness is our path of Zen.

"Heaven" is a macrocosmic word, implying the universal. The microcosm—that which is within our awareness—is a reflection of the macrocosm. Thus, Heaven is not only very far away from us, but also a state within us. Therefore, however important the bodily posture may be, formless attention is more so.

* * *

> There are more things in heaven and earth, Horatio,
> Than are dreamt of in your philosophy.
> (*Hamlet* I.v. 195–196)

Our bodies both reach up and penetrate downward. Often, when we think of reaching up, of ascension, we think of rationality. However, thinking only rationally bogs us down and stops us from reaching as high as we might. At the same time, we don't descend deeply enough, because our rational faculties stimulate our all too conscious willfulness, and, therefore, leave us cramped and shallow.

As I touched upon earlier, physiologists talk of the central and autonomous nervous system. The central nervous system governs sensory perception and the muscles we consciously control. It is strongly allied with rational thought. Whenever I think, "I am moving my arm," it is already moving. The autonomous nervous system, however, is not subject to our will: we need to familiarize ourselves with it.

Therefore, when we meditate, and sink into the space of the pelvis, we experience a fundamental rest, because our muscles aren't forcing themselves. We don't keep ourselves upright through our will or muscles, but through our skeleton—settled on our sacrum from which the spinal column rises. As well as an ascending power along the spine, there is also a descending, tranquil force. The more you surrender yourself to the downward motion, the better the upward movement—the movement from heaven to earth. As much as you let yourself go, the more naturally the upward movement rises by itself—leading to a purer inner perception.

Let us take the quotation from Shakespeare's *Hamlet* and contrast it with "In the beginning God created Heaven and Earth." Previously, I said that, at the beginning, the "One," the indivisible God, divided itself. Usually, we understand the word "one" to be a numerical value. But if we use "one" as a description of the Ultimate, it takes on a meaning of fullness so dynamic and overflowing that simply thinking of "one" as a number is poor in comparison. The unity divides itself and from our fragmented condition of being human, we open up avenues to that oneness.

What "There is more between heaven and earth" suggests to me is that, even if we attune ourselves and become one with the Earth, our body, and open up towards Heaven—keeping both side by side—there will still be many more phases of experience in between. For all those experiences in between, I want to use a term from the New Testament, namely "Heavens," (the plural of Heaven). This word refers to the heavenly regions or spheres.

On Earth, we perceive everything with a three-dimensional consciousness. The German Jesuit, Father Hugo Enomiya-

Lassalle, however, once spoke of our awareness of being as a fourth dimension of consciousness, a further stage of being human. The experience of a fourth dimension, or even multidimensional levels of awareness, reflects something of the biblical Heavens, namely the ascension into a greater fullness. The same considerations operate in reverse: for example, when you project an object onto a flat surface it loses a dimension—moving from three to two. In a similar way, we too can be projected downward from the Heavens, which are multidimensional, into our three-dimensional space. There is a descent from fullness—in which something is lost—and there is an ascension, in which an ever-growing fullness is added.

These considerations have a practical impact upon Zazen. When we talk of focusing upon the One, it is not a question of achievement. As I said, the road is hard. We have to pass through "the narrow door" (Luke 13:24), on the narrow path. Indeed, at the very moment we relinquish our thoughts, emotions, and everything else, we end up feeling straightened. We seem to have lost something. In fact, the opposite is true. By letting go of our fantasies and daydreams, we find ourselves in a greater space. That initial sense of limitation, however, is necessary for us to concentrate upon the One, through which we can attain a greater fullness. Only by releasing the very thoughts that continuously revolve within us can we do this.

Yet, we can never call this acquiring of greater fullness an "achievement." That word suggests that we've used our reason and willpower. These faculties are linked wholly with the three-dimensional world. Through being seated in Zazen for hours on end— hours that make a tremendous physical and mental demand on us—we may think that simple endurance and overcoming discomfort will somehow *earn* us enlightenment. But this kind of thinking never works—because our feeling of "crampedness" will only get worse. What is much more important is refining our thoughts and paying attention. Cultivating this kind of awareness—one that always precedes surrender—I would like to call "admission."

When we feel certain pains in our body, because we're feeling cramped, it's important that we distance ourselves from them and focus our attention on the specifically painful area. We aren't totally absorbed by our pain and don't lose ourselves in it; but we still accept that we have a part of our body that's in pain and need to take care of it. This is what I mean by "admission." We are aware of the painful areas of our body; but we are also aware of those parts that don't hurt. Therefore, we circumnavigate, as it were, the whole body with our perception.

But, we must equally experience ourselves as "thinking." When we become aware that we are thinking or feeling, we create a distance between the thought or feeling, and cut off our identification with it. Only through the "admission" of our thoughts can we relinquish them. This distancing helps us deal with our body and our mind in a subtler way.

In this way, we are prepared for that multidimensional fullness to which we, who are seated in Zazen, are on our way. On the one hand, our consciousness becomes one with the Earth, on the other, it reaches open to that ultimate fullness. Through all these stages or dimensions of descent and ascent, our awareness becomes multidimensional, until the ultimate fullness of all dimensions—which at the same time is Supreme Oneness—is attained.

* * *

He has us seated in the Heavens. (Eph. 2:6)

This citation describes in many ways a Zen *sesshin*. Of course, we are seated on the ground. But that hardly describes the situation, because our being seated needs to have a heavenly character. This means we must be centered on an objectless clarity, something we might call "heavenly," however painful our posture might be. Yet, the citation does say "Heavens," and the term does suggest something of the different phases we need to pass through in our consciousness. It is an ascent that gradually comes about through being seated in Zazen.

Throughout history, there have been thinkers who have tried to chart the heavens. Paul, without further explanation, states that he was taken up into the third Heaven (2 Cor. 12:2). Revelation also speaks of being carried up into Heaven (Rev. 4:1). From Jewish Merkaba mysticism (the mysticism of the Heavenly Chariot)[1], we learn we must pass through seven heavens to stand before the countenance of God. Dionysius the Areopagite talks of nine choirs of angels. While I'm not going to speculate on the truths of these claims, I bring up these examples to point out that they illuminate our own way through the various phases of consciousness.

---

[1] H.C. Moolenburgh, *A Handbook of Angels* (C.W. Daniel, 1988)

We can use several criteria to recognize these phases. First of all, we could look at how a deeper dimension is projecting itself into the everyday, three-dimensional reality we live in. For example, when we see someone behaving compulsively—washing his hands several times an hour, for instance—we surmise that the compulsion is concealed in the deep recesses of that person's consciousness. These causes, rooted perhaps in a hidden trauma that has molded this repetitive behavior, may never be revealed to that person. Just as the mold will endlessly produce copies of a similar shape, so will the trauma manifest itself endlessly in the sufferer's behavior. Again, when someone has been hurt in a relationship, the hurt communicates itself to all those whom that person meets. Time and again, the person feels things going wrong, until they become aware of the experience that caused their pain. Once more, the cause of the pain is placed on a deeper level than the surface reasons would seem to suggest.

Psychic Edgar Cayce once said, "Mind is the builder, the body the result."[2] To me, this means that when we construct things in our mind, we see the results of that construction in our bodies. There is connection between what happens to our body and our consciousness. As our meditation becomes more refined, we come across the molds that lie in the deeper levels of our consciousness. These molds belong, like our dreams, to a different level of awareness. On this level, everything is possible, as the visionary language of Revelation describes. Here, Christ reappears with seven stars in his right hand. The seer falls to the ground, and

---

[2] Herbert B. Puryear, Ph.D., and Mark Thurston, Ph.D. *Meditation and the Mind of Man* (Virginia Beach, VA: ARE Press, 1999).

Christ touches the seer with his right hand, lifting him up (1:16–17). The text does not say that Christ first laid down the stars to free his right hand—nothing of the sort. This is visionary language, which does not follow the logic of our physical reality. What matters in this passage is that there is another reality in which images blend and become transparent, just as in a dream. It is a symbolic reality.

In the process of meditation we gain a more refined awareness, in which we become one, as it were, with symbolic, visionary images. We trace the negative images within us and learn to release them, and, at the same time, unfold ourselves to positive forces.

While Zen is imageless, it is not somehow removed from the world of rites and symbols. Aside from strict Zen meditation, it is equally important for meditators to learn to use positive, creative images and symbols. In this way, for instance, in our monastery a link is forged between meditation and choral prayer, which is laden with holy images. While this positive connection is important, at the same time we need to track down our automated negative responses and learn how to abandon them. For example, if I think continuously about my work, I won't succeed in surrendering myself until I discover and let go of my need for self-preservation concealed underneath. The same goes for all images we come across in our meditation. It is not enough to relinquish the external when there is not that more refined abandonment of more deeply seated soul-images at the outset. We first have to admit our images or complexes to be able to relinquish them. After that, we can open ourselves up to the positive images the good is shaping in us.

* * *

Faithful Love and Loyalty join together,
Saving Justice and Peace embrace. (Ps. 85:10)

This sentence describes a kind of party of heavenly forces. I consider this verse to be a characterization of the next stage of awareness. The lowest heaven is the one of visionary, symbolic appearances. The middle heaven is the level of energy paths and divine forces. The transition between them only comes about when we've arrived at a complete standstill—when we have experienced the destructive forces of existence, for which the Bible uses the term "the wrath of God." When this happens, we're unable to advance and come away empty-handed, like Israel after the destruction of the Temple.

To experience the negative images we're dealing with here might provoke a feeling of impotence: "Where do I go from here?" As a result, we, as it were, unfold before the heavenly energies that flow through us. In the tradition of Zen, this "flowing through" is called *zanmai*, and constitutes a form of introspection in which the separation between object and subject disappears. In the lower heaven the contemplating subject still occupies himself with objective images. This now drops away. After the moment of *zanmai*, we realize we've reached a state of oneness and that the separation between object and subject has disappeared. In this state, we don't know we're meditating and it is only afterwards, when the gong strikes for example, that we notice we've passed through something, caught by something larger than ourselves. This experience was long known to the ancient monastic world. The monks knew that as long as you remained conscious of your prayer and meditation, you weren't really praying or meditating. In Western mysticism, this state is called a prayer of silence or intentional contemplation. These states are moments of oneness in which awareness of time and pain vanishes. Afterwards, when you realize the state you were in, you feel the joy, renewal, and power it gives you.

It is much better not to stop in front of the experience we go through in Zazen. We should be aware that the same experience of oneness can come about in daily life. We always need to remain aware of the relation between Zazen and daily life, because in daily life you too can experience that you are being carried by a force not your own. For example, it is often hard to bridge divisions in our society or within oneself. We often feel torn apart. Yet, there is sometimes a peace or harmony within ourselves that allows us to hold ourselves together and be authentic people—to be ourselves and not our smaller "I"s. Indeed, that power for peace makes us an instrument of something much greater than our individual selves—we become an instrument of peace and harmony.

This inner power has manifested itself in those who have struggled for peace and justice, for something they themselves can hardly handle. These people pursue their goals for years on end propelled by that larger force, to which they have surrendered. The same force is present in those who endure great suffering—whether facing a terminal disease, or feeling powerless, or languishing in prison. There is a force that carries them along and shines on those with whom they come into contact.

This force also expresses itself in the material world. God created Heaven and Earth. In doing so, He allowed Heaven to become visible in matter. Likewise, He made it possible for the material world to become transparent or translucent for those on the heavenly energy paths. In meditation, we gain a deeper awareness and unity that can make it possible for us to become, in our everyday lives, an instrument for the energy sources in the middle Heaven.

* * *

Eyes within and without, eyes in front and behind.
(Ezek. 1:18, 10 and 12; Rev. 4:6, 8)

The phrases in the above citations refer to the wondrous creatures called cherubim. The tradition of Dionysius the Areopagite perceived the third, upper heaven as the place where cherubim, the visionaries, and the seraphim dwell.

The cherubim have eyes within and without, in front and at the back. Because of this, they have an all-encompassing perception, a pure inwardness, in which the one who sees and the one who is seen coincide. As medieval mystic Jan van Ruysbroek says: "To gaze upon what we are, we are what we gaze upon" (*The Blinking Stone*, 2nd Vol. II A2). This is what, in Zen, we call illumination.

In the first half of his statement, Ruysbroek points out that we see what we are. What he means is that we behold the essence or meaning of our being. In the second half, Ruysbroek tells us that such introspection expresses itself in being. What this means is that, on the Zen road to objectless inwardness, there is no end. As soon as we think we have mastered the method, we objectify it and our small "I" emerges again. This is a deeply rooted inclination in us. Zen and the unadulterated Christian traditions agree on this: as long as we cling to an image or method, we create a boundary at some point and the movement is broken. We must constantly remain within the flow of contemplation, of pure inwardness. While we do need some sort of method, in which images play their part, we should not encase ourselves in images or the flow of objectless, multidimensional perception will not be allowed sufficient space to emerge.

This all may sound somewhat ethereal, and in some ways it is. The Bible has a word for this: Splendor. Splendor is radiation or pure light. It is very ephemeral, like the cherubim and the visionary. In connection with the cherubim we can once again talk of *merkaba*, the Heavenly Chariot. The Heavenly Chariot appears in different parts in the Bible and symbolizes the irresistible force with which God's spirit or invisible being whirls through matter. In Judaism, the Heavenly Chariot was linked to the Temple, because its rituals guaranteed the continuation of the physical world. The continuation of the world derived from the rites of the sanctuary, which expressed the divine power. That way the Temple carried meaning for the entire cosmos.

We now arrive at the next step, a deeper lever where the Chariot tells us everything about the temple *we* are, the temple of our body and being. In the Asian tradition, there is the term *chakra* in this context, which translated also means wheel or cartwheel. The chakras are, as it were, the whirling of God's force, by which God whirls inside of us. The different heavens, the different dimensions of existence, are not just layers on top of each other, but they penetrate each other, linking to connected levels.

These connections take place through relay stations where the vibrations of one level are transformed to those of another level. In Asian traditions these relay stations are called *chakras*. The chakras are often receptacles for patterns in which the energy expresses itself.

There are people who experience a kind of breakthrough by using drugs or because of brain damage and energy is suddenly released. That energy flows through the chakras, but is unable to find a way to express itself anywhere in new forms. As a result, nothing actually happens, the experience passes, and the person hasn't changed. When there is only the observation of the discipline, there is then only "fulfillment of the law" and nothing much happens. On the other hand, there are people who are so dedicated to observing spiritual practice and discipline that they forget the practice has to be an expression of force. Because energy and form relate to each other, we must be sensitive to that relationship on every level of consciousness—sensitive to the way that energy expresses itself in the forms and patterns we live in. The intangible characteristic, the clarity of introspection, needs to take shape within our body as well. That's why being properly seated is so important and is given so much emphasis. This is not a matter of form itself, but of the consequences of that turning inward.

Through the chakras, there is a movement both downward and upward, a descent followed by an ascent. Such a movement is traditionally called the golden chord, leading from the spinal base upward, and it is known as the Kundalini force. This ascending force is taken up by the descending one, which in the Bible is called the flame of the Pentecost. In the proper posture, the force becomes a stream heading both up and down. But in order for this to happen, the head and back must be erect, as in the text: "May the blessing be on the head of Joseph." (Gen. 49:26) You can hardly imagine Joseph with a tilted head when he was being blessed!

So it's vital that we feel the upward moving force rise freely and spontaneously, and at the same time open up to the force that descends from above. Then our whole being is like the cherubim's: eyes in front and at the back, within and without—pure perception. We behold and are gazed upon. At the same time we are lifted beyond ourselves and know we are safely lodged in the vision of God that encompasses all that exists.

* * *

The god who answers by fire is God indeed. (1 Kings 18:24)

These words are spoken by Elijah on Mount Carmel as a sort of formula of recognition. They are a challenge to the religious person who is prepared to make a sacrifice, but does not yet know how it must be sanctified. Elijah tells the priest that it is a heavenly fire that lights the sacrifice. In this passage, the fire refers to God's glory as well as to the sacrifice that must be sanctified.

After the cherubim, I want to dwell on the seraphim, who also dwell in the highest Heaven. For there are, as it were, yet more levels. According to the tradition of Dionysius, the seraphim, who do nothing but sing "Holy, holy, holy" (Isa. 6:3), are mentioned in the visions of Isaiah as the seraphim, or the "burning." They are called this because they are the symbol of both God's fiery holiness and sacrifice.

Contemplation becomes possible, and the experience of illumination appears, only when we "die the great death" and surrender the "I" completely. Likewise, it is only possible to persevere on the path of objectless meditation if there is, on the one hand, a readiness to sacrifice, and, on the other, the confidence that sacrifice will be sanctified. The sanctification does not come about from a fire you light yourself, but with a fire that comes from above. While the ascending Kundalini force exists, realization only occurs when the Pentecostal flame descends.

I am reminded of Paul's text, where he talks of Christ "who has gone through to the highest Heaven" (Heb. 4:14). Added to this image is that of the Temple—the courtyard, the sanctuary, the Holy Place (Heb. 9:24). But how does Christ enter the Holy Place where God is—for this has been sealed off with the veil of our consciousness? We feel that we live with a veil, the Ultimate is yet not accessible, and we ask ourselves: "When shall the curtain be drawn aside?"

The answer is that the curtain will be drawn aside ultimately through the sacrifice of our lives. It is not until this has been completed that the quest may find its end. The power to walk the path of objectless meditation is the readiness to sacrifice the "I." Even so, objectless contemplation is necessary to ensure the "I"-lessness," the sacrifice. There are people who, religiously touched, have not reached those profound depths of imageless contemplation, and remain somewhat "I"-bound. Contemplation cleanses the "I"; and at the same time the sacrifice of the "I" brings contemplation to its most profound realization.

The story of Elijah—"the god who answers by fire is God indeed"—is also found in the first chapter of the second book of Maccabees. The story goes that the priests hid the sacrificial fire in the mountains after the destruction of the Temple. The Temple had been ransacked, destroyed, and the people forced into exile—itself a representation of our own lives. After three generations, the people returned to the Holy City and the Temple was rebuilt for the sacrifice. Not knowing how to rekindle the sacrifices, they remembered that they hid the ritual fire in the mountains three generations before. The order was given to find it, and when they found the place, there was only brackish water. Nevertheless, they took the water and sprinkled it on the sacrificial animal.

This episode points poignantly to a deeper reality within us. When we are turned back from estrangement, we find only brackish water. This is an image of the pain we have to endure such as when, for instance, we're confronted with disease. Yet, this brackish water is poured over the evening sacrifice and, at that moment, a fire bursts from heaven and consumes the sacrifice. This fire relates to the "I" we're going to lose, the "I" that, as it were, is constituted by the manner in which we lose it.

By way of an example, reflect on the image of the cross. There is a vertical line and a horizontal one expressing depth and height. The vertical line represents the deep vital forces grounded in the earth and the higher forces to which the cross points. The horizontal line represents the self that must learn the worldly task of loving. Upon this junction of latitude and longitude, the self is consumed. There the fire of God penetrates the heavens and the "I" is sacrificed. But, precisely because of the force of the sacrificial fire, the "I" that loses itself is provided the task of realizing itself in this world, to carry its full responsibility and to love selflessly. The "I" is exactly the crossover where the sacrifice must be met.

The God who answers by fire, is God; when the fire consumes the sacrifice, God is there.

❦

10. The Path is the Body

"You have a body, don't you?"

THERE IS A ZEN STORY, OR, MORE PRECISELY, A Zen Christian story about the body. During his first Zen *sesshin* in a Zen monastery, Father Hugo Enomiya-Lassalle, whom we mentioned in the last chapter, asked his first Zen master or *roshi* Harada, whether he, as a Christian, could attain illumination. Because of that "silly" question, the Zen master looked very surprised and answered: "You have a body, don't you?"

Illumination has nothing whatsoever to do with Buddhism as a religion, as a totality of rituals and convictions. It has nothing to do with any particular race. It is only concerned with the fulfillment of human potential.

You have a body, don't you? You're human, aren't you? As a human you are equipped with a body and you are able to attain enlightenment.

* * *

95

The body is the most universal collective we possess as humans within our species. At the same time, it's the most personal. We can ask someone not to touch us or invite them to touch us. While the body is something we all have, whatever our race or sex, the body, precisely because we all have one, appears to need no further investigation. But Father Enomiya-Lassalle explicitly asked for illumination. What mattered here was realizing inner potential, which to be sure is innate to the body, but yet not obvious or easily realized. The Buddha was very unusual among human beings in realizing this state of enlightenment.

In that sense, Roshi Harada's reaction is comparable to Paul's when he was asked: "Is it possible for gentiles to become Christians?" This question arose because Christ was a Jew. So, ran the complaint, if gentiles wanted to become Christians they first needed to become Jews, which meant they would have to take on all the doctrine and rituals of Judaism. Even circumcision, inherent to Judaism, had to be a part of it. Paul replied, however: "Gentiles have a body just as Christ had one" (cp. Gal. 3:28). Christ had realized the primeval human potential of death and resurrection—both profoundly human because our body harbors life and death. Because we have a body, we live, and there will also be a time when we must die. But, in Christ, death has become resurrection—Christ has unified and realized the two primeval human potentialities of life and death. Through Him, the body can flower into the resurrection.

The Buddha realized another human potential. He showed us how, instead of allowing the body to drowse away, sink into forgetfulness, ignorance, desire and hatred, we can wake up and become enlightened. It is essential for us to allow both potentials to unfold within their own setting—settings which may not be so very far apart. As I have said before, in the Zen tradition mention is made of the need to die the "great death" to reach enlightenment. Having a body enables us to attain enlightenment, and this process of life and death is enacted within the body.

At this point, I would like to return once more to the manner in which we handle our body, or the practice of being seated. As I mentioned before, when we our seated together, in the posture required by Zazen, we know we are being asked to descend, ground, and earth our bodies. Yet, at the same time, we must ascend to the heavens. There is in this paradox a tension: for only when we really feel at home here and are well grounded, resting firmly upon the earth, can the body be upright. The sacrum is very important in this. We need to imagine that the sacrum is connected with the bones with which we rest on the earth. It is no accident that the last bone of the spine is called the sacrum, or "sacred bone." There is no *ritual* meaning to sacredness in this contest (even if ritual, as far as I understand it, is better appreciated in Zen monasteries than in the West, with our secularized frame of mind). Sacredness here is the primeval power by which we live. It is the power that supports us, just as the sacrum shores up the spinal column.

Sacredness here is also a transcending force. For at the same time the sacrum enables the body to rest, to be rooted, grounded, upright, and erect, it allows movement upward—of transcendence and heavenward ascension. This is the meaning of sacredness: a primeval force through which we exist, but which simultaneously transcends us.

In the polarity of "going to Heaven" and of "grounding," we unfold ourselves to this force of sacredness. The image the Bible uses for this is the symbol of fire, which denotes inexhaustible energy. But something else resonates in the image: anyone who handles fire carelessly is in danger of being burned. Worse, fire may also kill. Although today we might use the image of electricity rather than fire as a source of indispensable energy to us, the deadliness of high voltage cables still illustrates the danger.

What matters here is admitting the primeval power of God's holiness. And the emptiness we move into is no bloodless, weak vapidity, but is charged with the power of God's holiness, a force of life and death. It is a power within our body, within that tension of Heaven and Earth, that unfolds the potentials of illumination and resurrection.

"You have a body, don't you?" Be conscious of the potentials you are carrying within your body!

Meditation and the Body

Buddhism and Christianity have fully developed teachings about the body. In Buddhism there are three bodies: the *dharmakaya*, which is the absolute body of truth; the *samboghakaya*, the transformed, illumined body; and the *nirmanakaya*, or incarnated body. These constitute the three phases of the body of the Buddha and, therefore, everyone who follows the path of the Buddha. In Christianity, we speak of the body of Adam, the psychic "I"-body (*soma psychikon*), and of the body of Christ, both the crucified and the glorified body. The believer is baptized into that body, and in this way becomes a part of it. As is evident, archetypal symbols play a substantial role in both religions.

Is it possible to determine from the viewpoint of meditation what the body is going through?

The body of Adam, or so-called psychic body, is the "I"-body, the body that is our particular identity, different from everyone else. Becoming an "I" is a stage in our development that we cannot avoid, Yet, through the formation of the "I," the innermost or higher Self is lost. This Self is the association with the whole, the unity of God. As a result of our development, a fragmentation into separate "I"s takes place.

When we meditate, we notice the fragmentation in our consciousness, through the continuous flow of images that pass through us. However, when we start paying attention to the images that return frequently, we realize they are charged with emotional forces and manifest our fears, desires, and aggression. Simultaneously, in order to grasp on to reality, we develop ideas using our speculative self. Then we make the next discovery, namely that the emotionally charged images are connected with tensions and a feeling of "crampedness" within our body.

Our willpower fixes itself between our raised shoulders, and, in our wariness, we crawl, as it were, behind those raised shoulders. Aggression expresses itself through our muscles, for instance in our shoulders, upper arms, jaw, or throat. We suppress the feeling in those parts of the body out of sheer anxiety, because we fear our aggression. As a result, the tension within our muscles is doubled. The situation might be best described as trying to speed up and slow down at the same time. We'd fall apart if we allowed ourselves to be carried away by our desires. Yet, when we cut them off, pressure builds up in the midriff and obstructs the flow of our breath.

Now it might be asked whether dedicating oneself to attaining the right posture implies that we have to suffer an additional measure of feeling cramped. Or it might be the case that our body becomes a mirror in which we learn to see how our alienation reveals itself. Whatever way you look at it, however, during meditation the fixtures within our body—the instinctive bondage of the "I," the aggressive resistance, and the frightening tensions—are revealed. During meditation there is the wondrous interplay in which bodily posture, breath, and the emptying of the mind all perform their own part. We might define this interplay as follows: finding the right balance between tension and relaxation, learning to surrender the flow of breath, systematically refusing to entertain the images that appear to us, and recognizing the connection between these three. For example, obsessively thinking about the blockages in our body may be a sign of severe wounds we may have received in earliest childhood, and it is sometimes necessary to use other forms besides meditation to become aware of our body or eliminate blocks in our psyche.

What matters after all is said and done is that we get fully in touch with those forces that connect us with the whole again. In so doing, the piecemeal work of conceptual thought is replaced by intuitive observation, with which we observe the whole. We become more able to carry the burden because we know that we are supported by our innermost being. We know that our body no longer solely belongs to our singular "I," but has become a part of that One Body that conjoins us all, and which all Christians participate in: the Body of Christ.

The Process of Transformation

In the progress of meditation we all know periods of gradual development, inner repose, and peace. Repose and peace are all well and good, but they can be dangerous, for we might try to cling to the peace we have acquired. Furthermore, it is possible that all sorts of vague thought-patterns of which we are barely aware still exist in our mind. Sometimes, we have doubts we are barely conscious of and yet which exercise their influence upon us.

What needs to be done in such situations is, as they say in Zen, to use the "sword." (It's an image familiar in the Scriptures: "It cuts more incisively than any two-edged sword" [Heb. 4:12].) This image parallels that of the dying of the self, of dying the "Great Death." Before the Body of Christ becomes the resurrected body, it is first the dying body. The transition that takes the "I"-body—the body of our everyday selves—to the resurrected body is not gradual. Instead it involves discontinuity, a letting go of the old pattern.

In the Christian tradition, we are familiar with the image of the seed that falls to the earth and dies before it reappears as a crop, whether a plant or shrub. While the seed was indeed predestined to mature into the crop, it still had to leave behind its initial, particular body and had to dissolve itself into the fertile soil it was sown in. This is the image that Paul uses when he is asked what the form of our raised body would be (1 Cor. 15:35). We are still a seed, an acorn for example. We do not yet know how the full-grown oak will look. Yet, there is a continuity between the acorn and the oak, even if it is not a rapid or commonplace connection. For before one becomes the other, there has to come about a process of disintegration.

The natural world supplies us with yet another way of thinking about this. The caterpillar weaves itself into a cocoon to become a butterfly. What, we might ask, happens to the caterpillar that cocoons itself in this way: Does it experience resistance, does it have a sense of fear or even feelings of guilt because it simply leaves its former shape as a caterpillar behind? Biologists have noted how enormously radical this metamorphosis is. Nothing of the caterpillar remains behind except a few brain cells from which the genesis originated, a process of recombination of old fragments that accepts a new destiny together. Suddenly the sluggish, crawling caterpillar reappears as a light-feathered butterfly that flies toward the sun. The freedom of movement and beauty of the many different species of butterfly allow us in nature to gain a glimpse of what might be possible in a similar process of transformation.

To release our thoughts, desires, passions, anxieties, fears, disillusion, and depression all require a genuine process of dying. It requires tremendous dedication and courage as well as supreme attentiveness to allow this death to happen to you. You don't know where you will end up. All you know is that it is good to go through this process, with only the promise of transformation, resurrection, and a new life to entrust yourself to.

For clarity's sake, it would be a good thing for us to focus on the fact that we experience a physical as well as an inner, mystical death—even though, in truth, the latter cannot be separated from the former. It is only after the final passing away that the fullness of the resurrection may occur. After the mystical death, a breakthrough of the new life force may take place.

During the pupation period, we gain an inner transparency and sometimes a sparkling, intuitive brightness that deepens the perception. We grow more forbearing, because we feel supported in our innermost being, and we become more and more selfless and encompassing in our love. As soon as we leave the torpidity of peace behind in meditation and push forward to the utmost effort of dying, then a transformation superseding all expectations will take place.

* * *

This is my body. (Matt. 26:26)

Jesus's expression at the Last Supper reveals the sublime act of love with which He gave Himself to the very last fiber of His body. To His disciples, Jesus' declaration and gesture were the very signs that He would continue to gather them together, through both His particular and universal body.

A similar conjunction of particularity and universality applies to pain. For a start, pain in one's body is deeply personal, because we cannot escape from ourselves when we are suffering. We are constantly thrown back upon ourselves. Although somebody else might be near us and empathize with us, we cannot share that pain and that person cannot take it away. Nowhere are the limitations of compassion more profoundly revealed than when we are confronted with the unbearable suffering of someone else and cannot take it away, and nowhere is this suffering more acute than in the extremes of physical suffering.

Jesus expressed this suffering through His ultimate act of love. He prepared for this suffering during His temptation in the desert by Satan. In extreme purity, He learned to choose His Father, His beginning, and His destiny. Both experience in the desert and the suffering on the cross are intrinsically bound to each other. In between, lies Jesus' active resolve for His fellow men: proclaiming, healing, and liberating.

With the Buddha, it seems as if death is not described as the ultimate act of love so much as the final entry into peace, into the divine emanating stillness. In the Buddha's sublime act of love we see exemplified the struggle to break through into illumination. In the Buddha's own struggle with a tempter, in this case Mara, the latter—seeing how the light within the Buddha could no longer be contained—offered him a kind of illumination that would mean disembodiment. Buddha, suggested Mara, would be able to enter the light, *Nirvana*, but would no longer be able to have any dealings with the Earth and mankind. In this way, Mara could then continue his rule over mankind.

The Buddha refused to do this. He felt that the tiny piece of earth on which he was seated and on which he had fought his quintessential battle, entitled him to the entire Earth, the whole of mankind. His enlightenment was not just meant for himself, but for all creation. From now on everyone could share in the possibility of illumination. That is why the Buddha, in his moment of illumination, is always depicted gesturing to the earth with his hand. In enlightenment, a claim to the Earth is made true, and, in the forty years following his enlightenment, the Buddha proved that claim through his teaching.

What that means for us is that, while meditation is a process of inwardness, a thrust into enlightenment, it is not disembodiment. On the contrary, the body is taken along with us. The body is the battleground where the fight for pure, stilled attention takes place. Every blocked passage in the body must be converted into a self-releasing transparency—and the body provides the authentic seal. The body has to experience everything, undertake everything. In our bodies, we stand before and against ourselves, and can become truly and ultimately our innermost self. This is why being seated plays such a tremendous role in meditation.

As it turns out, through the Buddha pointing to the earth and Jesus' statement "This is my body," what is more particular and most intimate—namely our suffering—becomes the most universal through the fruitfulness of compassion. When the Buddha pointed to the earth, he changed it. When Jesus stretched out His arms on the cross, He changed the body of everyone.

Paul expresses this most poignantly in his allegory on the body. Every member of the body has its own singular, inexchangeable function. The eye sees, the ear hears, the feet walk, and so on. Yet, in his allegory, each particular part of the body engages in a sort of self-glorification. The eye elevates itself because it thinks only sight is important. The ear considers itself most important because it thinks only hearing matters. Yet the body shows that every individual function exists for the whole, and that outside of the whole each part has no purpose at all. The members of the body are inescapably dependent on each other; what they do for each other gives meaning to their individuality. In meditation, this tension is brought out very sharply. In sitting still, everyone is thrown into himself and the posture of meditation warrants the confrontation of everyone with himself.

Yet, as we sit together in stillness, we also sense how we mutually support and stimulate each other, how the silence of each of us is a supporting force for the other. We learn to focus our self-esteem and ambition—those qualities by which we try to prove ourselves—as a sacrifice for the other. We understand that what we are going through has to be fruitful for the other person, for only through showing compassion for the other person will our own enlightenment acquire meaning and fulfillment. After I have gone through the final confrontation with myself, I discover the essential solidarity that links me with the other person. And the body is the expression of both the confrontation and the solidarity—the final boundary. Through saying "This is my body," Jesus offers Himself and everything He has experienced. This is why He represents the totality of all things to all people—In the correct posture this may also hold true for us.

One way to understand this is to look at two different types of people. Some people keep well away from their body. They're inclined to lock themselves into a kind of inwardness, a kind of ivory tower mentality. Practicing meditation—actually sitting down and doing it—is very important for this type of person in order to test whether their inwardness is a genuine presence and not mere intellectualism. Only by coming home to the body, as it were, will the inward-focused attentiveness become an alert sense of presence, and at the same time be spontaneously transformed into compassion.

The other type of person is someone who is extraverted. They concentrate so much on other people that they completely ignore themselves. To such an extent have other people become the purpose of their existence—they want to help other people and dedicate themselves to them—that they are unable to turn within. For these people, practicing the inner path means breaking this compulsiveness. They must first learn to get acquainted with themselves in order to test the genuineness of their involvement with other people. The body must become a touchstone of inward attention. Only then will their compassion become a release for others as well as themselves.

Both the observing, detached individual and the compulsive, helping personality must pursue—through their body—their own path, in order to attain a liberating authenticity. Every human being must learn the profound significance of Jesus' words: "This is my body."

11. Words of Jesus from the Sermon on the Mount

Blessed are the pure of heart, for they shall see God. (Matt. 5:8)

IN THIS QUOTATION, SPOKEN BY JESUS DURING THE Sermon on the Mount, Jesus reveals His program as teacher of wisdom and righteousness. The statement is a striking reflection of how sight and purity are bound together—especially when focused on the Ultimate, God. There is something revolutionary about it. Not only is purity transferred to the heart but perception is contained in and expressed through the heart.

For the Pharisees, purity was connected with ritual. They believed that by dint of the rite you became pure and that ritual was the best way to see God successfully. Jesus disagreed. He said that it was not a matter of ritual—no matter how beautiful and exalted the rite may be. It was the heart, the essence of your personality, your consciousness that mattered. Jesus' declaration in the Sermon on the Mount contains something antithetical, which comes up more explicitly further on in the Sermon. Jesus brings up the contradiction between the act and source it comes from:

the inclination of the heart. He indicates that it does not matter how important the deed portends to be, whether an expression of righteousness or upkeep of the Ten Commandments; this, like a rite, is only the penultimate phase and not the ultimate. You do not reach God by it. Instead, something must happen in the heart, in the consciousness.

What does it matter, Jesus argues, that you don't murder someone or commit adultery if you still have hatred in your heart and your eyes are filled with desire? It's certainly praiseworthy not to perform the act, yet it is still only prefatory. For, when it comes to God, the Final Cause, you need righteousness of the heart and purity of consciousness. Indeed, sometimes the penultimate can be the staunchest enemy of the Ultimate, if only because it is extremely tempting to stall there and not move on.

The word "antithesis" here conveys something of the struggle inherent in this situation. We might think that there is something slightly delicious, and nice and quiet, about sitting in meditation. If you think that, you're wrong. Actually, if you sit down and begin to think you can take things quietly, all kinds of thoughts, all those thoughts we'd rather not face, emerge. Suddenly, your hatred and desire appear as large as life in front of you, and the struggle with them—the difficult battle you must fight before you can break through into the Final Cause—cannot be avoided.

If we compare Jesus' Sermon on the Mount with the Buddha's Four Noble Truths, they seem to be of the very same tenor. Only their point of departure is different. For Jesus, the starting point is that point before the Ultimate, of acting morally. He notices the danger of stalling there and neglecting one's inner composure.

The Buddha formulated his teachings about the Ultimate in relation to the actual human situation. According to the story told about the Buddha, when the Buddha left the royal palace in which he had been raised in total harmony, almost in a sort of paradisal peace, he had a number of encounters. First, he met an old man whose body was horribly disfigured by old age; next he met a man yelling, whose groin was diseased by black plague; and finally he came across a funeral procession which, with loud lamentation, was escorting a corpse to the funeral pyre. Later, the Buddha defined the shock he had experienced at seeing these events: that human existence is nothing but uncertainty, misery, and agony. This was the First Noble Truth, called noble precisely because it is true.

The Buddha then asked himself the question that forced itself upon him and does so upon us: What is the cause of this suffering? The Buddha's answer became the Second Noble Truth: The cause of all suffering is ignorance, hatred, and desire. Our tiny "I" sucks at the surface of material "reality" like a leech, without ever really knowing what is real and opposing everything that disturbs its insatiable passions. Each individual act of ignorance, passion, and hatred automatically leads to another one, one word follows another, and one state of consciousness produces another, creating an unending rope that ties us down. This is human existence.

After mercilessly confronting this situation, the Buddha formulated an outlook that could deliver us from this situation. It became the Third Noble Truth and announced that the chain of ignorance, hatred, passion, and suffering could be broken. The final step, the Fourth Noble Truth, asked the question: How will this breakthrough come to pass? The answer was the Eightfold

Path: The chain could be broken through appropriate conduct, appropriate speech, all the way up to appropriate attention.

It is the last facet of the Eightfold Path that became a developed feature of Zen. In Zen, appropriate attention means that you are able to stop your mind, break the chain of your thoughts, passions, and hatred through disciplining your attention. The life of the Buddha is itself a manifestation of disciplined attention. Sitting under the Bodhi Tree, the Buddha in total concentration conducted his ferocious battle with Mara, the god of illusions and passions. The Buddha struck at the heart of true understanding, pure knowledge, and complete contemplation—possessed of a purity that brings us back to the passage from the Sermon on the Mount. What matters to both is a struggle against our thoughts, a drive into a purity, a sheer inner attentiveness.

Zen has developed the method of appropriate posture and correct breathing to support the path of inwardness and anchor our consciousness in the purity in which the Ultimate of God may reflect itself. Rites are allowed, good deeds are important, but ultimately all that matters is the process in the recesses of our heart where our consciousness is stilled and the purity of introspection is realized: "Blessed are the pure in heart for they shall see God."

* * *

Do not let your left hand know what your
right hand is doing. (Matt. 5:3)

This again is one of Jesus' beatitudes from the Sermon on the Mount, in which He warns us about the danger of pious practices such as prayer, giving alms, and fasting. Although these are beneficial in and of themselves and naturally focus us on God and our fellow beings, they must not be taken possession of. If we do so, we fall into the very subtle and discordant pit of inward, spiritual vanity that comes when we show off our piety. What matters is an inward unity, which is as valuable as inner purity.

Jesus' symbol in the quotation above is one of two hands. The statement suggests that there is duplicity or discord within the consciousness—one caused by self-reflection. What Jesus is pointing up is that beyond the self-reflective consciousness where the speculative mind no longer penetrates there is an inner unity that is created in the unseen. It is the place where the mystery of our own essential nature and the mystery of God come together.

Let us begin by examining the twofold nature of the hands literally. In opposition to the binary nature of our hands stands the unity of the spinal column. Fanning out from the spinal column we have two upper legs, two upper arms, and after a double bone in the arms and legs, five carpal bones, tarsal bones, and toes on both feet. Jesus doesn't make it that complicated: He only speaks of two hands. But this shouldn't stop us from considering the symbolism of the skeleton, a unity that branches into a multiplicity.

The spinal column as a symbol of unity is often compared with the tree of life. In a suitable posture and thus erect, our spinal column gets the opportunity to become a tree of life, rooted in the soil and focused on Heaven. One must also become well rooted in the right posture, solidly rooted in the ground. Through the nutrients of the soil, the tree of life bears fruit, which is itself a process of reshaping and transformation. In the Bible, you find the symbolism of the rod of Moses, by which he performs his miracles. This rod has always been thought of in connection with the tree of life, even though it has practical uses as well. To us, thinking of the spinal column in this way shows how valuable it is. It is, of course, self-evident that the tree of life branches out into an abundance of twigs that carry fruit. But, our spinal column also needs hands and feet to balance the diverse circumstances of our life.

That's not to say that abundance is wrong. It only proves wrong when we are unable to attain an inner unity in our consciousness. Our ability to contemplate induces the ego to look at itself and to dwell on its own image—something that leads to vanity. When we look at ourselves in a mirror, we allow ourselves to recognize who we are. But we should not simply linger on the surface and seek pleasure in appearances. We need to press on.

What goes for pious practices applies in some ways to meditation. Both demand an enormous effort and great quickness of mind. For one thing, given that it is not easy to find the appropriate inner posture, it's logical that my rational faculties pile themselves on top, as it were, to observe everything. But the result is the opposite of what was intended.

By way of analogy, consider cycling, skating, or dancing. These activities suggest an inner balance. When you are self-conscious or not relaxed, you never get the hang of them. Likewise, when you do start to get the basics, you find yourself wobbling somewhat at your own efforts. It is not at all easy, this struggle against self-reflection and vanity. But it is nevertheless very necessary—especially when it comes to true holiness and meditation. This is not only because vanity actually repels true holiness and meditation, but, above all, because it stops us attaining inward unity. Because of pride, we are unable to enter into the mystery of our innermost essence where we start to realize something of the mystery of God. We experience this mystery as a sort of immersion in which the fragmentation of time and space fall away. The ancient desert fathers said: "As long as you know you are praying, you are not really praying." As long as the left hand still knows what the right hand does, there will be no coordination!

Now you might be wondering how one can compare meditation with movement, given that meditation appears to demand stillness. The short answer is that the movement exists in our breath. As soon as we stop in self-reflection before ourselves, we immediately notice our breath. We have to be conscious of the movement of our breath—but it is a consciousness that is a very subtle listening to the actualization of our breath, a perceiving that does not objectify. The consciousness must never become fragmented into merely the ego wanting to do it all by itself or seeking to draw itself closer to the results. As you can imagine, this attentiveness—the kind needed to enter into the mystery of God—needs to be very nuanced. It is, we might say, a conscious concealment—although this time it is on the level of God. Jesus says: "Your Father who sees into the hidden recesses." When we arrive at this mystery, our ego, during many of our deeds, will no longer be the thoughtless core but will yield to the real midpoint of our existence: the God that perceives the innermost secrets.

* * *

Behold, look at the lilies of the field the birds in the air, and wild flowers, do you really perceive them? (cp. Matt. 6: 26–34)

This is a question Jesus wants us to focus on. If you turn from meditation to the world around you, the external reality, you notice that your perception becomes clearer. It has always struck me that the drawings made by Zen masters and artists reflect such a pure vision. The inwardness of Zazen is one that opens you to the perception of beauty around you.

Jesus' inquiry is here primarily directed at people that worry. Obviously, people who worry tend not to perceive anything around them, because they are engulfed by their worries. The desert fathers note that it is difficult to come to terms with worries when they occupy our mind. I think that if we were to keep track of the kinds of thoughts that whirl in us during meditation, a great deal of our reflections would consist of worries.

It is not, of course, because worrying in itself is wrong. Indeed, a caring that comes from compassion is a blessing when it is a question of caring for others. But very often anxieties entrap us. Now, obviously, somewhere, something has gone wrong and something is occurring in our innermost being—again, this might not be such a bad situation to be in, since we might be able to release our thoughts, and continue on: the journey inward is not always linear. Indeed, we simply can't just throw off our worries the same we do our clothes and be the same person underneath as when we were clothed. We are transformed.

What are anxieties and how do they affect us? There are, of course, many different forms of anxiety, each casting its own shadow. You have very pressing anxieties, possessive anxieties, anxieties about parenting, anxieties because of injuries—all of these types of anxieties show us something about our worries. Anxieties point to a relationship between the emotions. In itself, this relationship is positive, as long as it does not shut us off from the end point, which is the final fullness of existence. When we are greedy and act possessively with what was given in our care, our anxieties cut us off. Anxieties belong to the world of having.

When the monastic fathers want to talk about anxiety they talk of "greed" and "seizure"; because anxiety ultimately contains a longing for something we want. As soon as this desire arises, the fear of losing what we want arises, too—the desire and the means to thwart that desire are coexistent. This paradox is actually the reason that it is so difficult to surrender our anxieties. Greedy, frightful anxieties can increase the distress in our consciousness so that the beauty of nature eludes us.

To Jesus, wild flowers and birds are an image of God's beneficence. God feeds the birds and clothes the flowers. The questions are then: What do wild flowers and birds reflect in ourselves? What do they say to us about the proper, innermost dimension of our existence?

First, they offer us receptivity. Whereas anxieties tend to bog us down in the dimension of having, birds and flowers initiate in us something altogether different, something new, namely the domain of being. Instead of our exhausting efforts, there is an openness that makes it possible to be nourished in quite a different manner. The Bible uses the word nourishment in a profounder sense than taking bread—for "man shall not live by bread alone, but by every word that proceeds from the mouth of

God" (Matt. 4:4). Secondly, following on from receptivity, the birds and flowers offer us clothing. Again, we are not talking about external clothing. It is the clothing of the self-esteem from our faith, the knowledge that we are children of God, the God who takes care of us.

All our deeds, choices, thoughts, and emotions constitute, as it were, a cord of life. Will this hemp be spun by laborious plodding or by courageous confidence? In biblical language, the garment is a representation of the inner life: In the heavenly spheres the martyrs are clothed in white robes (cp. Rev. 7:9). The thread of life we have spun will eventually determine our final garment. Will our robe be the result of our own covetous efforts, or will it come from God's gift, freely given? Wild flowers and birds teach us what we are in our innermost being: children of God, called to irradiate the luster of God's Kingdom.

* * *

Blessed are the poor in spirit. (Matt. 5:3)

This declaration begins the Sermon on the Mount. It is a programmatic judgment. Reading it, we're forced to confront the opposite of poverty, which is wealth. In Saint Matthew's Gospel, true wealth is that by which you are saved. When Peter hears about the rich man who like a camel tries to wriggle himself through the eye of a needle, he retorts: "Yes, but if even the rich cannot be saved, who will?" (cp. Matt. 19:23–35) Wealth here is obviously the element that will save you, by which you are going to make it. As long as you don't see the leather of your pouch, you might say, you're going to make it.

Jesus is not addressing the plight of the material poor in the utterance, "Blessed are the poor in spirit." He is talking about a still deeper poverty—the poverty of the mind, a profounder level on which it is important not to try and succeed on your own. For this is truly what Jesus meant with this beatitude: It is very important not to make it on your own, not to get it done, for only by surrendering your efforts and receiving the kingdom as a gift can the fullness of happiness and joy be attained. When we look further into the Sermon on the Mount we come across another illustrative declaration—a statement in which Jesus, with excellent conciseness, endows His words with unmatched powers. This assertion runs: "judge not" (Matt. 7:1); or, in a parallel text of Luke: "Do not judge, and you will not be judged; do not condemn, and you will not be condemned" (Luke 6:37). Being judged and condemned are obviously the consequences of judging and condemning.

This is, in many ways, a terrible, almost gruesome declaration by Jesus, because we consider judging to be a normal activity of the mind. If the mind can no longer do what it is usually employed to do and which seems natural to it, is there, we might ask, anything else that can be done with the mind? In the statement, we notice that judging and condemning are put together. Both facets, as it were, are the riches of the mind belonging to an autonomous human being. As long as I am able to judge and, in the nature of things, also condemn, I still know who I am, because that requires judgment.

Think of a child on the beach. In itself, the beach to a child is uninteresting—vast and shapeless. Yet, build a sand castle on it, and the child knows exactly where she or he belongs, which spot is his or hers. That is why a child builds a castle and the sea rolls over it and the child builds the castle anew. We are like the child. We build our own castles in order to know who we are, drawing our moats to protect ourselves from others and establish our boundaries. In this way we judge and condemn at the same time.

So, judging and condemning constitute an activity of the mind—but it is an activity that is emotionally charged, since we ascribe value to our judgments: "I am not like that other person. The other person is wicked and I am much better." I need that other person not only to know myself, to know who I am, but also to make me feel better. If that other person wasn't there I wouldn't be able to think myself superior! In this way, the judgments of the mind are loaded with emotional and moral values, and it is precisely these values that endow the mind with enormous power. For it is not solely a question of a mental activity. What also matters is the image of myself in which I have invested in my life. And I assume God recognizes this, too. In our arrogance we presume that, although we know that God exercises judgment, He would really agree with us. And yet Jesus tells us not to judge or condemn.

I will ask again: Does this signify a denial of the mind, of our autonomy? Not in a negative sense: the possibilities available to the mind are God-given, willed by God, meant by God, and it is not necessary to deny them. They may no longer be decisive however, for they must be embodied in a larger whole. For example, every piece of stone in a mosaic is singular. If, to remind us of Paul's analogy, the stone were to claim that it was the only important stone in the mosaic and that the remainder had simply no value whatsoever, the mosaic would no longer be a mosaic. In the mosaic every small stone is important, all that matters is the whole; yet it is a whole that is nonetheless differentiated, with a singular place for every pebble.

Both the analogies of the stone and the body show us how impossible it is to exist outside or loosen ourselves from the whole. And, more to the point, when we experience ourselves as part of the whole, judging and condemning lose their restrictive and stultifying influence. The boundaries become relative and so can no longer be regarded as absolute. And, in a further surprise, when we live from the whole, we discover ourselves. This is really what the metaphor of the body seeks to demonstrate to us. The liver, for instance, is precisely the liver because it is part of the totality of the body. It does not find its identity by distancing itself from another organ, but acquires it through its relationships. This suggests a new consciousness developing itself, namely a sense of intuition, where one has knowledge of the whole. It is no longer a matter of saving ourselves through judging and condemning, which in the end will only result in adverse effects. For the judgment we pronounce on others will always fall back on us. People who reject one another often feel they are being rejected by others.

So, the questions remain: How can we open up to that wholeness, from which we exist and through which we can really start to function and fully be ourselves? How do we unfold for the whole? In what way does the breach become the line of communication?

This is a delicate point, one open to misinterpretation. We could talk about it in an agreeable way, or even become enthusiastic about it, but we must remain aware that becoming fully ourselves within the whole means a dying to ourselves, a dying to the singularity by which we vindicate ourselves, by which we intend to make it. Only in this way may we become aware of the whole surrounding us, carrying us, and giving us a purpose to live for. That is how silence becomes a source of life, a new consciousness.

The poet Guido Gezelle, a Flemish Catholic priest, expressed it exquisitely in his poem *In Speculo*:

My eyes shall see you once,
sated and faring as the drop,
smothered in the ocean:
it shall see You, groundless in the throes of the sea,
perceiving, with neither rim nor resting place.

The sea has become seeing!

* * *

Love thy enemies. (Matt. 5:44)

The phrase is again a testimony from Jesus from the Sermon of the Mount; and again it is a very characteristic expression. Jesus does not say it is pleasant to have enemies or that you're not allowed to have enemies. Jesus assumes we have enemies and gives us guidance on what we should do about them. Jesus says that we owe something very special to our enemies, namely the prospect of love. And it is a love that is more fully embracing than the uncomplicated love that comes spontaneously.

The Dalai Lama also speaks of accepting our enemies, but he expresses it somewhat differently: "Your enemies are your best tutors." This is a very radical statement, especially coming from someone who has endured so much suffering, who was expelled from his country, and is forced to live far away from his own people whose religion and culture have been totally annihilated. And yet he says: "Your enemies are your best tutors." The emphasis in this declaration is laid above all on "tutors."

Jesus emphasizes the new possibilities offered in the confrontation with our enemies: the prospect of a love that transcends all human boundaries, in which something of God can become visible. Jesus tells us to "be children of your Father in Heaven" (Matt. 5:45) and "set no bounds to your love" (Matt. 5:48)—something seemingly impossible on the human level. For Jesus, what matters is not the ethical, moral purpose of perfection, but something that comes from God, which at the same time might be called mercy (cp. Luke 6:36). The picture Jesus paints is that of a Father who makes the sun rise over the good and wicked (Matt. 5:45). God does not think: "These are evil people, they don't deserve it." When it comes to good and evil, God transcends our human boundaries.

Let's rephrase the questions: Where do our enemies come from? Where does evil come from? These are typical, human, intellectual questions—ones we like to think we could solve if only we knew the causes. We like to believe we can control matters better than God (in our opinion) is doing; for God seems to allow evil to exist and even He, according to Paul, has enemies: "For if, while we were enemies, we were reconciled to God..."—a wonderful expression, our guilt is atonement—"...we shall be saved through His life" (Rom. 5:10). God needs no help: He knows how to deal with evil and with enemies.

An enemy obviously enables a special revelation of God's love, so the question is not where evil comes from, but where it leads to. What is the purpose of the difficult, given reality of an enemy? When we enter the silence, we not only encounter the enemy and the emotions that person calls forth in us, but we are also able to push forward to the divine prospect hidden deeply in us and to love our enemy. Through us, God wants to reach the fullness of His creation, for He desires to restore its wholeness. That this is a process of learning, as the Dalai Lama says, is obvious. And here is another example, taken from the Bible. The moment Solomon abandons God, he topples as it were from his fullness, and there arises against him an adversary (the word "Satan" in Hebrew—1 Kings 11:14).

In the Sermon on the Mount, Jesus tells us that we first learn to love in our small, trusted circle, but afterwards we are called to grow into a love that embraces everything and everyone. In practice this is a difficult learning process, which, sometimes, at first means we need to learn to stand up for ourselves and muster a little fighting spirit, but only as much as this struggle is not beset by any bitterness and unfolds into attempting to measure oneself truthfully against others.

Once again, I must reiterate: All these admirable words of wholeness and the all-embracing must be tested, up to the very limit. Light is only light after passing through the dark. Love becomes only love through confronting your enemy, and it is the enemy who enables the final breakthrough to the essence of God—a love that in turn desires to manifest itself through us.

❧

12. *I is not I*

HERE IS A DUTCH ANTHOLOGY OF THE
Buddha's writings translated by Tonny Kurpershoek-
Scherft, published under the title *There Is No Self* and
subtitled *Buddha's Message of Happiness*. The sentence "There is no
self, no existing I" is, I believe, a very good characterization of the
Buddha's message and his teaching.

I deliberately make a distinction between the Buddha's
message and his teaching, since it is almost certain that Buddha
was very practical and only wished to point out a path of life
without establishing a philosophical system of learning. Consequently, "There is no I, there is no self" is surely very characteristic of Buddha's "message of happiness," notwithstanding the
manner by which it has been elaborated in successive philosophical systems. I believe, for example, that when Dürckheim
talks about "the little 'I' and the large self," he opens up a degree
of perspective through which we can approach this paradox and
experience the observation that "There is no I, there is no self."

Jesus, too, made observations about the "I" and His own self, and they are not much less paradoxical than the Buddha's assertions handed down to us or recorded by later schools. In one episode, Jesus answers those people who are astounded because of His eloquence when He supposedly had not received any education: "My teaching is not from myself" (John 7:16). In this assertion, the paradox is brought to the fore. Instead of "My teaching is not my teaching" we might just as well say "I is not I."

What matters is the "I" in the teachings of Jesus, the way in which the people receive them. To those who admire His personality but simultaneously ask critical questions because of it, Jesus says "My teaching, my 'I,' is not my teaching, is not my 'I.'" Or, to be more precise, "My teaching is not from myself: it comes from the one who sent me." I is not I—I is the one who has sent me, the Father.

At this point, let us compare some statements:

Jesus declared publically: "Whoever believes in me believes not in me but in the one who sent me, and whoever sees me, sees the one who sent me." (John 12:44–45)

The message is obvious: I am not I, but the Father. Does this mean that Jesus is only an illusion and that His preaching is also? No, at least not in the sense that the "I" of Jesus disappears. But the affirmation stays the same: He who sees me or my teaching sees Him who sent me. The endorsement of the "I" remains, but at the same time it is denied. I think it is important to endure the particular tension of this paradox, to refrain from choosing a one-sided solution by eliminating one of the opposites of this tension.

In the fourteenth chapter of John, we find a text more familiar to us. In response to Philip's question "Lord, show us the Father," Jesus replies: "Have I been with you all this time, Philip, and you still do not know me? Anyone who has seen me has seen the Father" (John 14:8–9). We might make the quote more comprehensible by saying: "He who sees Me, sees not Me, but the Father." A little earlier, Jesus says: "If you know me, you will know my Father, too." (John 14:7)

So it is perfectly clear: all these observations contain a relationship of Jesus with the Father and a relationship with Jesus and His audience—between Jesus and those who are addressed by Him, who hear Him, and have seen Him. That way there always exists this two-way relationship: Jesus toward the Father, and Jesus toward those that listen to Him.

* * *

When our group meditates, the question often arises among the monks how, while we wish to be silent and enter the stillness as much as possible—to be, in a certain sense, in relation to the silence, the inwardness, alone, and avoiding contact with each other—we are still together. How we solve this paradox is by recognizing that we are not meant to reach out for all kinds of contact, but need to be attentive toward each other. We need to cultivate an attentiveness in which the other person is taken up. And all the while, there is that stillness that hints at the abyss we're looking for, that innermost reality we open ourselves up to, and to which those manifold thoughts, emotions, and impressions that our small "I" (as stated by Dürckheim) has is an obstacle.

Buddhism also teaches that the "I" is an obstruction. Buddhism unfolds the "I" in diverse aspects: through the body, feelings, impressions, thoughts, etc. In the original texts attributed to the Buddha you find only five layers of the "I." In later texts, each of these aspects of the "I," which in fact isn't really the true Self, are elaborated upon. This is observable within the stillness of meditation. As long as we are trapped within the aspects of the "I" that cannot be the true Self, we are unable to sit still properly and our breath will land us in difficulties. There will be a barrier somewhere, and Jesus' expression—"I is not I" (and "not I" is then the Father, who has sent Me)—remains an unrealized potential. We must continually break through these barriers by which our "I" is impeded, release the things our small "I" instinctively clings to. We must break away from all of this, to allow that ineffable stream to flow through us.

With the help of several citations, I would like to go somewhat deeper into this matter. We have already noted the observation: "My teaching is not from myself: it comes from the one who sent me." The text continues:

> Anyone who is prepared to do His will, will know whether my teaching is from God or whether I speak on my own account. When someone speaks on his own account, he is seeking honor for himself; but when he is seeking the honor of the person who sent him, then he is true and altogether without dishonesty. (John 7:17–18)

He that speaks for himself—let me reiterate for the sake of clarity, from the small "I"—seeks his own glory. Here a particular criterion is being established, a certain aspect in which, as in Buddhism, all the aspects of the "I" which are not the true self, so therefore an illusion, are expounded. In this instance, only one criterion is given, namely seeking one's own glory, or remaining fixed within the aura of the "I" returning unto itself, locked in a closed circle, completely tied-up in self-reflection.

That situation needs to be overcome so it might become open for the true glory. "I is not I" is the manifestation of what might occur within us while we are meditating.

Not of My Own Accord

There is no systematic analysis of the "I" in the Gospel of Saint John, the phenomenal "I" as in Buddhist philosophy. There is no summary of every aspect with which the personality expresses itself and through which we experience a sense of identity. Yet some aspects are pointed out, and in these circumstances it is striking that the stress is laid on "working." Indeed, I might go as far as to say that in working or in undertaking some task or activity, the notion of the "I" is extraordinarily strong. Working gives a strong sense of self-determination.

In the fifth chapter of the Gospel of Saint John we find the story of a paralyzed man who was healed on the Sabbath. The story actually concerns a man who does not want to be healed, for, although there is a healing source nearby, the handicapped individual does not really make any effort to experience its powers. And yet Jesus heals him; and asks him then, even on the Sabbath, by way of therapy to take up his own bed and walk.

I think of the paralyzed man as an example of "paralyzed contemplation." He just lies there, paralyzed. That is the reason why Jesus wants to teach him that lying still is not just contemplation. Part of contemplation relies on dedication and making an effort. This is why the man needs to carry his bed, even on a Sabbath.

Breaking the law of the Sabbath causes mutterings among the Pharisees. Jesus tells them: "My Father still goes on working, and I am at work, too" (John 5:17). This statement claims the very opposite of the Sabbath's rest and the wretched listlessness of the paralyzed man. Instead, it is a formula for hyperactivism. God just cannot stop working and nor, says Jesus, can He. Jesus equates His own activity and work with that of the Father, and thereby puts Himself on the same footing as the Father. This, Jesus consequently explains further on: "In all truth I tell you, by Himself the Son can do nothing" (John 5:19a).

Once again, there is the topos "I is not I." This time, however, the phrase is combined with the formula, "can do nothing." So, at the very moment of self-affirmation, every sense of the self, every experience or confirmation of its existence through activity, is being denied: "In all truth I tell you, by Himself the Son can do nothing, He can do only what He sees the Father doing."

What Jesus is making clear is that there can exist a sense of "doing" things, but it is one that is mediated through an experience of the self through the Father in a relationship—one established through perception and contemplation. Thus, contemplation and work, introspection and action, are fundamentally related, and the two extremes of wretched inertia and hyperactivity are transcended into a higher level. We might envision the involvement of contemplation and activity as of a key and a keyhole. They fit into each other perfectly: without one the other is nothing: "For the Father loves the Son, and shows him everything He Himself does" (John 5:20). As this quote exemplifies, while the Son may manifest introspection there is simultaneous showing on the part of the Father in a mutual involvement that, on the side of the Son, expresses itself in contemplation, and, on the side of the Father, is a presentation of Himself and an expression of His love.

(Incidentally, it is well to point out here that we shouldn't understand the expressions "Father" and "Son" as responses to a nostalgia for patriarchy or concern for living in a era of absent fathers. We should understand these words as the representation of an essential relationship, a fundamental involvement that touches life itself.)

There are still other descriptions that exemplify this same occurrence: first of all, somewhat further along in Chapter Five, we find: "By myself I can do nothing; I can judge only as I am told to judge" (John 5:30). The work discussed here is obviously judging; and, especially in connection with judging, not being able to act on its own accord is expressed in the concept of hearing—as it was expressed above by introspection.

In booklets about meditation you sometimes receive the advice to let your doing and your activity grow from your innermost essence, to do simple things such as washing up, typing, watering flowers, or something similar with such an attentiveness that you feel it is happening out of your innermost essence. The point is that it is not you who is doing the action but that the action is happening to you. It demands a very special attentiveness to let something occur to and through you. That is why it is best to start with simple things.

Jesus, however, as He makes clear here, does it with the most difficult thing of all—"judging," which means as much as "taking decisions." Those who have a managerial position and are accustomed to taking decisions and making judgments know from experience how much is required from their dedication and responsibility. Jesus lets this judgment, this making of decisions, continuously spring from another source, from what Jesus Himself calls the Father. And the attentiveness with which this takes place is called, in verse 19, seeing.

In verse 36, Jesus says: "The deeds my Father has given me to perform, these same deeds of mine testify that the Father has sent me" (John 5:36). This is quite a profound commentary. The Father is portrayed here as an employer (a very modern word!) in the sense of one who assigns work. This is a moral and legal relationship established in which the responsibility of the other person is kept inviolate. But this bestowal has yet a profounder meaning, becoming fully intelligible in the fourteenth chapter, where it is simultaneously a question of speech. Acting and speaking are always synonymous in the Gospel of Saint John:

> What I say to you I do not speak of my own accord: it is the Father, living in me, who is doing His works. (John 14:10)

In this way, the act of bestowing gains an even deeper significance. It is not solely that moral, judicial relationship: the work has been commissioned and it is up to the other to see how he will get it done. The work itself has been commissioned, which signifies that "the Father acts within me," it comes from yet a deeper source. But in that expression from that innermost source, my own responsibility and dedication are not being excluded, but come from a deeper place. The analogy is perfect. It is "not on my own accord."

We could state it this way: You receive an assignment from without and you have to carry on by yourself, at your own responsibility; yet the one who receives this commission is, I would say, like the clerk who, without knowing exactly what issue is at stake, is doing what he is being told to do. Or, a better analogy yet, it is as if he is a marionette being pulled by some strings and something happens.

Obviously, we're dealing here with a combination of work and being worked that exists on a deeper level. To the extent that action in which there is a strong sense of personal identity is rewarded, it is done in such a way that the "I" is not eliminated; on the contrary, on this level the "I" is being experienced in all its intensity and the relationship of continuously "seeing," "hearing," and "giving and receiving" issues from a profounder principle that here is called Father.

In the fourth chapter of John we find yet another expression. The question here is food. The disciples urge Jesus to eat food, but He replies: "My food is to do the will of the one who has sent me, and to complete His work" (John 4:34). To accomplish the work, which here is called food, is to Jesus a fulfillment, a state of being satisfied. It is through fulfillment that Jesus lives.

In the writings of Lao Tzu there is often mention of "not-doing" or "non-action" in order to get the work done. When we sit in stillness, we indeed feel an urge for activity that seems imprinted in our body. Then, it is a question of releasing that urge and from it propelling ourselves forward into the innermost essence from which that "doing" will be bestowed. In other words, we must always release the confinement of self-confirmation in stillness, the desire to do it ourselves and to grasp onto it. Instead, we must let it go to make it happen, to receive it from the essential foundation of being. Lao Tzu's term for not-doing, *we wei*, is paralleled by Jesus' "not of my own accord."

Origin and Destination

"I is not I" has been our point of departure. We have concentrated on the formula "not of my own accord" in connection with the work and preaching of the Son. The phrase "not of my own accord" actually points to the source. What Jesus is saying is that His origin lies somewhere else, which adds a whole new dimension to the relationship of "I is not I, but the Father."

This notion is brought up in a pericope in which the people are doubtful and wonder whether Jesus is really is the Messiah. They add: "Yet we all know where He comes from; and when the Christ appears no one will know where He comes from" (John 7:27). The people know that Jesus came from Nazareth and in that sense they know His origin. Yet they were aware of a legend in which they had been told that the Messiah would come without anyone really knowing exactly where He came from.

Jesus takes up this idea and gives it great emphasis. It says in the text that "He cried out"—it was, as it were, a cry from the essence—in the Temple: "You know me and you know where I come from" (John 7:28). He then adds a pivotal statement: "Yet I have not come of my own accord; but He who has sent me is true; You do not know Him, but I know Him, because I have my being from Him, and it was He has sent me" (John 7:28–29).

We already saw that the Son does nothing of His own accord. Now we hear that the Son has not come of His own accord. There are many meanings of the word "to come." Common words with a profound meaning are eagerly used in the Gospel of Saint John. The meaning of "performing" is much the same as to "come." You perform as a musician, comedian, director, or a professor. What matters is the particular role you need to perform, to fulfill toward others.

Well, then, in this role and performance, you are, Jesus says here, not defined by yourself. I, says Jesus, did not come on my own accord, but came from a different reality, from a different source. Jesus emphatically declares: "I know Him. There is really someone who has sent me and I know Him." Jesus experiences Himself as sent, as an instrument, as it were. He has a mission to complete in which He is defined by another reality He is familiar with, a reality He is totally aware of.

That awareness of origin—and that awareness is crucial—is balanced with the awareness of destination, as we find in the pericope that immediately follows. The chief priests have sent out their servants to catch Jesus. Jesus tells His followers:

> For the short time I am with you still; then I shall go back
> to the one who sent me. You will look for me and will not
> find me; where I am you cannot come. (John 7:33–34)

In making these statements, Jesus places His assertion in high relief. But He doesn't give an answer. Jesus' announcement is a kind of puzzle, a koan. Like the people around Jesus, we ask questions, questions which have a false bottom to them:

Where is He intending to go that we shall not be able to find him? Is He intending to go abroad to the people who are dispersed among the Greeks and to teach the Greeks? What does He mean when He says: 'You will look for me and will not find me; where I am you cannot come?' "
(John 7:35–36)

So, it remains a question, a mystery. What is important here is that Jesus speaks from His own solid sense of where He comes from and where He is going. In our daily life our notion of the individuality, of our "I," frequently restricts itself to the circumstances and situation surrounding us. For Jesus, however, there is an enlargement of this "I"-sense that reaches inward to the innermost source and outward to a final destination. And, what is the remarkable thing about Jesus, this is done with great certainty and utmost clarity. This feature is further elaborated on when Jesus testifies: "My testimony is still true, because I know where I have come from and where I am going" (John 8:14). The truth of Jesus' testimony is confirmed by the awareness of His origin and destination. It gives authority to His speech.

Finally, the same idea is brought up during the Last Supper. Jesus reiterates the same words, but now explicitly directs them at the disciples:

Little children, I shall be with you only a little longer. You will look for me, and, as I told the Jews, where I am going, you cannot come. (John 13:33)

Peter zealously wants to follow Jesus, but Jesus tells him that he can't, yet. Further on, Jesus says:

> You know the way to the place where I am going. Thomas said, Lord, we do not know where you are going, so how can we know the way? Jesus said, I am the Way; I am Truth and Life. No one can come to the Father except through me. (John 14:4–6)

Here we have the well-known pronouncement of Jesus in which He calls Himself the Way: He alone is the Way to our final destination. I am the authentic Way, He says, the reliable Way. I am also the path of life, the way that leads to Life. In other words, I am the Way, accessible for others, that others might go that way through me.

I believe these words about Jesus' origin and destination, about His whence and whither, are a widening again of the assertion "I is not I." Jesus' "I" widens to a certitude about His origin, and also widens to a bestowal, a total sacrifice of self in His destination. This destination also implies that unsolvable mystery for most of us: death. To Jesus, death has become a total self-giving, the sacrifice through which His existence widens towards us, by which He is wholly open, accessible to all. This way He invites everybody to find the reliable path, the way of life. Here, too, we have a two-folded relationship: Jesus toward the Father, and Jesus toward us. He is the way we may set foot on.

In the stillness, everything that keeps our small "I" confined to the unassuming situation of our task should fall away. Whatever commission we have been given or part we have to perform should, in its fulfillment, be a breakthrough to that dimension of being out of which we may become the instrument of our innermost source and profoundest destination, of self-sacrifice. We can be a way that is made passable for others.

* * *

"I Am"

When we Westerners observe Asian religions, notably Hinduism and Buddhism, from afar there seems little difference between them in our eyes.

However, the largest difference between Hinduism and Buddhism lies in their response to the statement "there is no self." Hinduism teaches the reality of *atman*. Atman is Sanskrit for the innermost divine Self, available in every human, and experienced by the Hindu as a sort of an individual, personal, and even divine unity. It is the divine essence every individual possesses. Buddhism, however, teaches *an-atman* or, in Pali, *anatta*: "there is no Self." It is difficult to know whether either observations are only metaphysical reflections or have something to do with practice. They touch on experiences we in the West might find hard to identify with.

Yet, when consulting the writings of yogis and swamis, you regularly come across the advice to meditate on the word "I am," which is entirely in line with the *atman* teaching. "I am" is a sort of sacred word, like a mantra, that allows you to penetrate your innermost essence. On the other hand, in Buddhism, and especially in Zen Buddhism, the slogan is not "I am" but *mu*, "nothing." Mu means nothing more nor less than "this is not what matters, that is not reality!" Everything that arises during meditation, every image and thought, every notion of the "I," is followed, as it were, by a blow of the hammer: *mu* is *not* that, *that's* not reality!

When we return to the Gospel of Saint John, we notice that "not-I"—not on my own accord—reappears continuously. It appears when Jesus is doing His works ("I can do nothing of my own accord"), when He is coming, and when He is acting ("I do not come of my own accord, I am sent"). To our surprise, we find at the very heart of these "not-I" utterances an expression of "I" again which, I would say, is charged with the greatest possible force.

Let me give you two examples, both from the eighth chapter of John. The final two words of the first example—"If you do not believe that I am He" (John 8:24)—are sometimes translated as "it is Me." It is a formula of acknowledgment, and when using such a formula we deploy the word "it." However, when you say "it is me," you must be able to insert something, a definite predicate, a specific "I am so and so," whereas nothing needs to be put down here. It is only a fullness of being, and in that sense our translation needs to be: "If you do not believe that I am" (John 8:28). To carry the paradox to extremes, the passage continues: "And that I do nothing of my own accord."

"Doing" and "speaking" are, as usual, paralleled by Saint John. Immediately after the term "I am"—in all its absoluteness—Jesus says, "I do nothing of my own accord." This shows two things. When Jesus is using the expression "I am," this is not the in-itself, resolved monad. It is not the man who, solitarily, searches his own innermost heart. To the contrary, the expression springs from his own receptivity toward the Father. Moreover, Jesus does not use the word to remain isolated within Himself, but to become a gift toward mankind. Therefore, the term "Son of Man"—a very mysterious phrase, found in the gospels in particular, that signifies the preeminent human—is used here. In order to make this point clearer, I will turn to the next formula. At the end of the eighth chapter Jesus says: "In all truth I tell you, before Abraham ever was, I am" (John 8:58).

This segment follows Jesus' claim that He comes from God and speaks the words of God, words that grant life. Jesus tells His opponents that they do not come from God, even if they say they do; that Abraham is not their father, even if they say he is, because they are focused on murder and lies; and that if it was true that God really was their Father, they would accept Jesus' words, because He *does* come from God. And then, as the profoundest expression, the innermost confirmation of that, Jesus says: "I am." Again, Jesus adds caveats:

> I do not seek my own glory; there is someone who does seek it and is the judge of it. (John 8:50)

> If I were to seek my own glory, my glory would be worth nothing; in fact, my glory is conferred by the Father. (John 8:54)

Again, as we have encountered many times before, we strike upon this undercurrent of "I is not I." My glory is not my glory, but the glory the Father bestows on me, not my honor but the honor the Father bestows on me.

This is fundamental for the Gospel of Saint John. In all sorts of keys, in every different shape, "I is not I" reappears continuously. Jesus speaks out of the "I am"—as pure receptivity toward the Father, but also as a confirmation to the people, to us. It is a relationship with two sides: a relationship with the Father, but also a relationship with us. And, through this, the figure of Abraham, Abraham the patriarch, is eclipsed. In the biblical mind, the patriarch defines his tribe, his offspring, and the people. The highest a nation may aspire to is the stature of the patriarch. Yet Jesus says: "Before Abraham was, I am." Abraham, says Jesus, was only a "becoming." Abraham, says Jesus, was focused on me and… *I am.*

That is also the import of the term "Son of Man." The "Son of Man" is the image that will determine human posterity, the new patriarch of mankind. This image attains its profoundest meaning in death: "When you have lifted up the Son of Man, then you will know that I am He" (John 8:28). In death, suggests this passage, *in extremis,* at the very endpoint of the pouring out of the self, the words "I am" may be pronounced. In this manner, and this is the most amazing thing of all, the strongest affirmation of the "I," the "I am," becomes a total gift: a total gift from the Father to us.

Here we touch upon the apex of the paradox: "I is not I" and yet again it is I. In this brief formulation, this phrase is plainly nonsense. However, when we learn to see the phrase in the progress of the Gospel of Saint John, it can lead us directly to the innermost mystery of Jesus' character, which is also a path for us. The "I am" is not denied, but is only made possible out of the "not-I," in which the true receptivity toward the Father may unfold and we in turn become a gift, bestowed on the other. So, in John's Gospel, the most profound meaning of the "I am" is this pure receptivity and bestowal, a gift in which, as far as Jesus is concerned, the fullness of divine presence is bestowed and the innermost divine warrant for Jesus' mission is given.

Because this formulation is also the expression used by God in the Old Testament—"I Am that I Am—the phrase arises time and again, whenever the fullness of presence, the ultimate warrant of God's workings in history, which shroud his I, is bestowed on us as a gift. And Jesus, out of this receptivity toward the Father, becomes that presence and warrant for us, out of the fullness of divine being.

Reciprocity

When Jesus talks about the Son and Father in the Gospel of Saint John, or about I and the Father, this automatically implies a duality. I and the Father, the Son and the Father, always make up two. But aside from this, there is only one passage in the Gospel of Saint John in which this duality as such is bluntly confirmed, even though it is, as such, implied everywhere. It is in the text I have already quoted, where it is a question of the truthfulness of Jesus' testimony.

Properly speaking there is something ironic in what Jesus is saying: "In your law [specially Jewish law, although this naturally applies to every other law] it is written that the testimony of two witnesses is true" (John 8:17). Jesus continues: "I testify on my own behalf, but the Father who sent me testifies on my behalf, too" (John 8:18).

Here we see that Jesus suggests that there are two. But, ironically, this duality is yet of such a nature that it has a tendency toward oneness. So, when the Pharisees ask Jesus "Where is your Father, then?", they are in a sense looking for another person, one separated from Jesus, who has to be present, on the spot, although not directly visible. Jesus' response is thus baffling to them: "You do not know me, nor do you know my Father. If you did know me, you would know my Father as well" (John 8:19).

Again, we see that the "not-I," and the visibility of that "other," of God, is really made possible through the "I-lessness" of Jesus. Through the "I-lessness" of Jesus the Son, the Father becomes visible. That way we arrive at the innermost meaning and the profoundest nature of that "not-I" in the Gospel of Saint John. Although it is a question of duality on the outside, as confirmed in this text, the innermost focus is not two, but *one.*

"Not two" is, I would say, one of the slogans of Zen meditation and the Zen mind: "Not two but one" bridges the antithesis and it does it through the "not-I," the "I-lessness." John confirms it everywhere: "The Father and I are one" (John 10:30).

* * *

One: this word is often interpreted solely as meaning a unity, as one thing—"The Father and I are one." In the entire pericope from which this quotation comes, this statement, however, stands as a confirmation of the fact that Jesus' life-giving work is one with the Father's; or, reversed, the Father is the ultimate redeemer, the innermost source of power of Jesus' life-giving work. Yet, formulated here directly at us human beings, at the closing of the tenth chapter, that pronouncement ("The Father and I are one") is somewhat rephrased:

Even if you refuse to believe in me, at least believe in the
work I do; then you will know for certain that the Father
is in me and I am in the Father. (John 10:38)

"The Father is in me and I am in the Father." This is just
another way of expressing the unity between Father and Son. In
this second formula the involvement and the relationship are
emphasized more in the nature of "The Father in me, I in the
Father." The meaning of this is that we are so at-one that we both
are defined by each other, that we exist by virtue of our
focusedness on each other.

By way of confirming this observation, in the fourteenth
chapter of John this formula is repeated to point out that the
Father is working and speaking through Jesus; so there exists, as it
were, a "not–I." But, Jesus reiterates, it is not I who am doing it,
but the Father in me who is doing it:

Do you not believe that I am in the Father and the Father
is in me? What I say to you I do not speak of my own
accord: it is the Father, living in me, who is doing His
works. You must believe me when I say that I am in the
Father and the Father is in me. (John 14:10–11)

But we need to go to the seventeenth chapter to find this
theme of oneness made even more explicit. The prayers in this
chapter are texts that have become very well-known through the
ecumenical movement. (Note here gain the word *one*):

I pray not only for these but also for those who through
their teaching will come to believe in me. May they all be
one, just as, Father, you are in me and I am in you, so that
they also may be in us, so that the world may believe it
was you who sent me. (John 17:20–21)

The unity between the Father and the Son is obviously
something that is passed on to the disciples and the faithful. To
reiterate, the innermost power of this unity is, I believe, that it is
an involvement of the personality, of I–Thou. I believe this
involvement is most adequately expressed by the word "bestowal":
the Father bestows works, the Father accords words, the Father
gives life. Everything that denotes welfare for humankind, that
which the Son accords to us, the Son has first received from the
Father. There is a continuous involvement, a relationship of
granting and, consequently, receiving.

In tandem with this relationship between Son and Father, as
well as us, the words "glory," "splendor," and "irradiance" emerge:
"I have given them the glory you gave to me, that they may be one
as we are one" (John 17:22). In passing on that glory, that
irradiance, a unity is established, which means that "I don't seek
my own honor, but the honor of the Father who has sent me" (cp.
John 7:18 and John 8:50).

As long as we are focused on ourselves in the things we do,
think, or feel, and have but our own image in front of our eyes,
we're seeking only our own honor and only self-reflection. But,
when that self-reflection falls away completely and we become
totally transparent, then that other reality shines through us,
enabling us to perceive in the Father and the Son the sheer

brightness of another reality. It is a reality that shines down on us, the faithful, as it shone on the disciples:

> With me in them and you in me, may they be so perfected in unity that the world will recognize that it was you who sent me and that you have loved them as you have loved me. (John 17:23)

Giving is an expression of love, it is love-in-action. It is the "not-two" of the Father and the Son expressed in the act of bestowal and receiving, in a cycle of love. I am firmly of the belief that this is indeed the deepest fulfillment of the "not-I" in the Gospel of Saint John. It is the "not-I" that penetrates the innermost essence, enabling the flow of love and irradiance of the glory. This is evident at the opening of Chapter Seventeen in John's Gospel:

> Now, Father, glorify me with that glory I had with you before ever the world existed. (John 17:5)

This pronouncement reminds us a bit of the question we encounter in Zen: What was your face like before you were born? Or, as is sometimes asked, what was it like a few generations before you were born? What matters here is the inmost irradiance of being. At the moment He dies, Jesus prays that this inmost irradiance of being shall be bestowed on Him again. The profoundest "not-I," which passes through death, is the expression of that oneness of love, which also allows the irradiance of glory. The "not-I" of Jesus, of the Son, such as we find in the Gospel of

Saint John, is the openness of being, which allows the emanation of love from the Father to become reality.

I believe I have shown something of what the Gospel of Saint John tells us about the "not-I" and the "not-two," and that it also makes us enter the path to stillness, to the emptying of self that may occur. When we meditate as a group, a unity becomes possible in which we admit each other. Yet that unity is something that takes place between God and us, between our innermost origin of being-and-love and ourselves. Yet, it also flows together, when we mutually absorb each other; that they may be perfectly one, even as "Father, you are in me, and I am in you" (John 17:21).

❦

13. Words of Jesus from the Gospel of Saint John

Destroy this temple. (John 2:19)

THIS PASSAGE IS ONE OF JESUS' ANGRIEST statements, spoken with all His zeal, fire, and innermost force, after He had tried to cleanse the Temple—the external temple of stone—of its outright mediocrity, ambiguity, and compromised position. When Jesus doesn't succeed, He observes that it is precisely this half-heartedness that will ultimately bring the Temple down. Tear down this temple, Jesus says: Destroy it. Ultimately, He says, you will bring it about yourself. Yet, Jesus notes, the destruction will not be the end, but, rather, a promise of something new. For "in those days," Jesus tells the people, there will be yet another temple. But it will not be a physical temple. It will be a temple at your disposal, the temple you are, the temple of the body.

"The temple of the body." This is such an inscrutable and profound phrase; and it touches on one of the most moving realities of the Gospel of Saint John, that is articulated elsewhere in a very short and almost condensed sentence: "the Word became flesh" (John 1:14). The most profound, the most original, final reality has become flesh and appears before us in a human shape. In such a phrase, the body becomes for us most human and, we might also say, the most divine.

It has always struck me that, especially in the Byzantine liturgy, there is so much veneration and awe, astonishment and reverence expressed for the incomprehensible and inscrutable mystery surrounding the incarnation of the Son of God. It is not that such reverence is exaggerated; it it awesome simply because it reveals itself as what it is: a mystery.

The temple of the body is us. At the very least, this phrase suggests to me that we need to give up everything we possess, all of the external ephemera. This may sound easy. But the same concept of giving up all we have applies to our innermost thought patterns as well, the ideals we devise in "having." Even our innermost inspirations must be relinquished as long as they arise in the form of "having." The fire of aggression that first focused itself on everything surrounding us and purified it, is now called upon to focus itself on the inside. We must die to ourselves, even pass through that abyss of nothingness, and learn to subject ourselves to the process of the Greater Death.

As I have suggested before, once this occurs then, eventually, something new happens to us. That new spirituality is not a disembodiment. On the contrary, in that newness, the body actually acquires its full measure. In the practice of being seated, in sitting still and not being restricted, in not adding energy to our efforts—because restriction really belongs to the domain of having—we are thrown back upon the dimension of being, through the nothingness and the dying.

I have noted already that stillness is an expression of pure attention. The purest attention that goes through us takes shape in the immobility of the body. In sitting still there is no longer anything we possess and no longer a diversity of thoughts. Instead, there is only emptiness within, a sign of our pure, undivided attention, of our receptivity. This comprehensive attentiveness is also expressed by our hands, as the hands are folded together in an expression of receiving. It is vital to understand that the composure of one's hands only expresses receptive attention. You should not lay your hands in a cramped position. The same applies for our pelvis. The open receptivity of our pelvis should be as an open bowl. All that matters is the quality of our attention. From it, we learn that we are the body—even in that divine dimension of existence.

* * *

Christianity and Buddhism draw our attention to the fact that the spiritual process is not a disembodiment. Our aim is not to become a ghost, or try and play a ghost, but to really accept our bodies and become earth. We Christians know this because the Son of Man descended deep into the earth and only then did He ascend, but without losing the earth in the process. In the same way, as I indicated earlier, the Buddha's hand, seated in illumination, always points to the soil.

That is why it is so important to be linked to the earth, with all our weight and gravity. We must feel how we rest upon the soil and are rooted in the earth. Only from this position will it be possible to straighten the spinal column.

Ascension and resurrection. Resurrection is not a disembodiment, it is resurrection; only then does the body appear in its authentic, truly intended, divine form, the Ultimate glowing through it. The Word becomes flesh, irradiating with the primordial, as the body that is you. As soon as you let go of the temple you possess, as soon as you start to realize that there are no solutions along the path of restriction but only through dying the Great Death, the body will appear in the true image that God intended. It is in this fashion we should treat the body and discover the body that we *are*.

Breath

As readers will now be aware, physical immobility is very important in Zazen. Breath, however, as I have said before, is movement. While we sit still, externally, physically, it should be as if we simultaneously become pure movement because of our breath. Yet, it is hard to release ourselves to the sheer movement of breathing.

When we ponder the saying from John's Gospel—"God is Spirit" (John 4:24)—it all sounds very static at first, mainly because we often link the word spirit with intellect and understanding, and think of it as opposed to matter. However, the expression "God is Spirit" really means "God is Breath." The sentence continues: "and those who worship Him must worship Him in spirit and truth."

While this is the literal translation, what we should say, rather, is that we must worship His reality in breathing. In such a way does Jesus tell Nicodemus that rebirth takes place through breathing, that through breathing rebirth occurs (John 3:5).

Nicodemus, as I touched upon earlier, represents the socially accomplished man. He is a person who has been successful in every province of life: because of his decent and observant life, his learning, and because of his rank in the hierarchy of government. In every respect he is socially successful. At the same time, however, he is also an inwardly unsatisfied man—someone with regressive thoughts, someone who wants to return to the womb of his mother.

Jesus tells Nicodemus that he must be reborn, to enter an entirely different dimension of existence. How can this come about, asks Nicodemus? Jesus tells him that the breath of God will make it happen, because God's breath is pure movement. In a similar way, we must surrender ourselves to the movement of that breath. Breathing is stopping to hold the self in our hands, manipulating and managing it. It is simply allowing the movement of breath within us.

Breath-Spirit. The word spirit certainly does not denote intellect here, even if consciousness has something to do with it. In the Gospel of Saint John the spirit is also called "the Spirit of truth" (John 14:17). The Spirit-Breath reveals and transports us to another level of awareness (cp. John 14:26), because breath and attention are joined with each other. But this conjunction does not take place on account of the mind, as the mind confines us to our usual consciousness. It occurs when we surrender ourselves to a force that is moving in us, inspiring us, and which we don't know where "it comes from or where it is going" (John 3:8). The force befalls us and we have to let it happen.

What really matters here is the spirit of truth, because the breath opens here a new consciousness, revealing a new reality to us. The breath has an enormous power. If we take stock of these words in the Gospel, referring to the Holy Spirit, the Holy Breath, then we can observe that it only comes after the earthly shape of Christ has gone (John 16:7). The coming of the Spirit, therefore, supposes a dying, a dying to ourselves, a dying to the external shape, in order to attain that new awareness.

The breath brings recollection (John 14:26). In the process of meditation, we receive a number of impressions we don't understand, but, through meditation, we begin to understand their proper meaning because the breath is connected with the subconsciousness, those layers of depth within us that may then grow into a new consciousness.

The breath also leads to the whole truth (John 16:23). The whole truth is not merely the discovery of something we can add to our previous knowledge. It is an entirely different dimension of insight. What matters is the process of transformation, one worked on by the breath. The Holy Spirit, the Holy Breath, brings us the whole truth. The Holy Breath also bears witness to a new confidence. While we may derive a sense of security from external sight and hearing, we now possess a different certitude, whereby we know for sure within us that we have found it. If the new awareness unfolds in us, we are confident within and have no doubt. The Holy Breath testifies, gives certainty, and proclaims.

"Testifying," "assuring," and "proclaiming"—these are words of revelation. Here the word "proclaiming" signifies "making actual." Directly, bypassing all concepts, and fully realized, God's Breath sets us in motion and our life's mission takes shape. God's Breath becomes a force within our breath, and the transformation begins. So, within the stillness of the body, there is the pure movement of God's Breath.

And there is nothing you can alter. It occurs to you, you are a spectator. You observe, as it were, from a tiny corner. However, if you observe too consciously, you are taking control again. And yet you need to observe, otherwise you drop out of that state. You must be alert and conscious so that it happens to you and you are taken along. But we must know that it is not we who move, but we who are being moved. It is not we who breathe, but the breathing of God's Holy Spirit in us.

"Behold the Lamb of God"

These are the words of revelation by which Jesus is introduced by John the Baptist in the Gospel of Saint John (John 1:29). Later in the Gospel we find Pilate's well known expression: "Ecce Homo" "Here is the man" (John 19:5). The significance of amalgamating these two statements about Jesus is that they show that the image the suffering Christ took on Himself for us is fundamentally human.

With Buddha, this is not so explicitly voiced, even if it does play a role on his path to illumination. Buddha endures all sorts of tribulations caused him by Mara, the Seducer. He goes through all sorts of suffering, and thanks to his persistence, evidenced in his suffering, he is able to break through into illumination.

We, too, experience suffering when we meditate together. To sit still is to turn oneself inward. Doing this makes us recoil from the inescapable suffering we all carry with us, each on his own path, in his own way. To one person, suffering is the agony of purposelessness; to another it is suffering caused by feelings of guilt and injustice, or from loneliness and feeling forlorn. Suffering manifests itself in everyone. We hit up against it when we are still physically as well, since, because we are seated, the body plays a large role.

Yet, even though we shrink from suffering, we have to deal with it. We have to learn to look at it and face the pain we carry within ourselves. We have to face the Great Death; a "death" that you feel intensely and experience when you set foot on the path of stillness, contemplation, earnestness, inwardness, and observation. When you travel on the path toward the light, you inevitably come up against agony and the only thing you can do is to observe it without repulsion. In other words, we have to accept it by perceiving the pain and thereby addressing it.

In that sense, it is necessary to admit we suffer. That is why the Bible speaks so emphatically about *beholding*—as in "Behold the Lamb of God." We come across the Lamb of God again in the Book of Revelation. There the book is also present (cp. Rev: 5:1) as a symbol for the history of mankind, every nation, and every human life. In Revelation, a powerful angel asks who is going to open and read the book, but no one does, and our story, contained in the book, obviously remains unread. At this point, Revelation tells us that the narrator weeps bitterly (Rev. 5:4) with a sorrow born of desperation, because the story doesn't appear to continue.

Yet there is one who will ultimately open the book, the book with the seven seals, which we might call the seven phases of initiation. It is the Lamb, standing sacrificed before God's throne (Rev. 5:6). Here suffering (the Lamb who is sacrificed) and resurrection (standing before God's throne) are combined, and this combination is what is essential. The suffering we encounter upon our path, has, to my mind, a divine quality, something of it that is God. It is fascinating to see how modern theology, in an intellectual fashion of course, puts forward the question whether, if God is suffering, God suffers or exposes us to suffering. It is not my intention to raise the question here as an intellectual problem, but I bring it forward here to show you how this question presses for an answer in man's consciousness. Our task, then, is to realize that suffering is a divine quality, whereby agony and resurrection, one way or another, seem to merge. Suffering and glorification, suffering and divine brightness—one way or another they seem to be effectively linked to each other.

* * *

What matters here is each and everyone's personal response to suffering and glory—and to understand their connection it is important to observe, learn, and see. In learning to observe we unfold that profound human, primeval cry that also may rise unhindered. Shouting and yelling are part of Japanese Zen. While we Christians don't do it as loudly, we still admit an inner scream or assent. The agony wishes to express itself in that manner; the ultimate quality of human existence wants to articulate itself that way; the ultimate quality of human existence wants to realize itself that way. That's the reason a great number of the psalms are filled with screaming—time and again, the primeval cry of human agony returns.

There are even passages in which God is represented as one who piles suffering on us: "For me He is a lurking bear, a lion in hiding. Heading me off, He has torn me apart, leaving me shattered. He has bent his bow and used me as a target for his arrows" (Lam. 3:10–12). These passages are ones in which the horror of suffering is depicted in its full horror, in images that completely take your breath away. Yet, at the same time, these depictions prompt us to face suffering, to accept it and live through it. In this manner, suffering is a final reality not detached from God, but something related to God. The finite and infinite collide with each other in a manner impossible to understand. The primeval collision of our existence shakes us to our innermost foundations.

Only in a stammering, searching, and groping way may we voice that this agony is in some way related to God, in some manner attaches us to the ultimate of our existence. That is why it is really a word of revelation: "Behold the Lamb." Mainly, it is a question of our own agony. Every human being stands on a place where suffering is unique. It cannot be transferred; it will always be my or your suffering. There is nothing that throws someone back so much on his loneliness than suffering and dying. We must actualize our own suffering and accept it. But, and this is the second step, when it is truly realized, there won't be a thing that connects us so much with our fellow human beings as suffering.

There is no better school in compassion than the acceptance of suffering. Mainly this comes about through our own suffering. Practicing solidarity with our fellow humans and learning to shoulder our sufferings is how we are able to carry suffering along with us. The significance of the Lamb of God is that we shoulder our own suffering, accept it, and subsequently learn to participate in the suffering of mankind, the world, and the cosmic agony. This is precisely why "Behold the Lamb of God" are words of revelation: Being seated, we allow this to happen to us.

Meditation and Zazen are a Process

The term used in the Gospel of Saint John and the Bible in general for the process paralleled in meditation and Zazen is "the way." "I am the Way," says Jesus (John 14:6), indicating that the process itself already has absolute validity and is not merely a means for an end, for then we would be able to manage and control it. No, the process befalls us, and that is why Jesus says: "I am the Way."

In addition to the term "the Way," there is yet another word that is used for this process in John's Gospel, namely "door." Whereas "the Way" chiefly applies to something that is long and maybe slow and arduous, "the door" points to the immediate—if you can imagine a door that suddenly opens. To be sure, the opening of the door might be preceded by a long lapse in time, a time in which the door remains constantly closed and we sit in front of it. The door might be opened just a crack. But there is a sense of immediacy, nonetheless. The images of "Way" and "door" show us different qualities of the process.

We might want to ask how we experience this process, how it is enacted before us, and where we emerge. We may worry about even raising these questions. However, when Jesus says "I am the Way," the process in itself is enough and no questions need to be raised. That the process is sufficient unto itself was the experience of Zen master Dogen, too, who handed down the tradition in Soto Zen. Dogen stressed that meditation in itself is already illumination. He said that the first half hour of being seated on one's cushion was already illumination, since it liberated you from your preconceived ideas, from "the attempt to realize something."

In Rinzai Zen, on the other hand, one looks upon Zazen as a path that will *lead* to illumination.

It is possible to describe the process as being from the small "I" to the larger self. In this formulation, the term "self" is a sort of code that can help us interpret an experience that cannot be reproduced in words, but which hints at our innermost identity. Whenever we become conscious of our "self," something crucial has befallen us and a process has been consummated.

For that consummation, the Gospel of Saint John uses the word "abide." The notion of "abiding" possesses an abundant richness of connotations, associations, and shades to make us experience whatever fruit this process might bring to us as a result of its development. "Abiding" comes from the pronouncement "I abide in you, as you abide in me" (John 15:4). The phrase characterizes the relationship of the Father to the Son and the Son to the Father, in which the Father is the principle of the unconditional, the absolute, and the all-embracing, and the Son is the principle of the tangible, the form. "Abiding" implies something both poised and continuous.

At the very outset of being seated, we are flooded by a torrent of thoughts because there is no stability whatsoever in our consciousness. We cannot see our thoughts, but if we did, we would see that our consciousness, under the impulse of our thoughts, is pushed in each and every direction, as in a whirlwind. But, as we go more intensively through the process of transformation, contemplation, and observation without judgment, more stability develops and we are truly tested. Whenever our thoughts go off in each direction, thirty minutes of meditation seems like it lasts forever. However, when our attention is composed and there is a sense of profound rest, the time seems to go quickly. Scarcely have we begun than the end approaches and we feel that we've acquired rest in our consciousness—rest, equilibrium, continuity, and a sensation by which our normal experience of time falls away and gains another quality.

There is also a sense of security inherent in the word "abiding." It is linked with the idea of "residence" and "dwelling": "I abide in you, and you abide in me." The word points to a dwelling with each other, a feeling of security with each other. When we meditate, the actual form really abides in the unconditional and absolute. The corporeal, measurable universe disappears and falls away, and in its place comes another, universe—one immeasurable and yet possible to inhabit. The Gospel of John offers various examples of the archetypal images of the Heaven that point to a universe of unending happiness. One's innermost heart, one's consciousness, becomes that dwelling. And, at the same instant of dwelling, we are also free.

There is yet another expression in John's Gospel, that is at once striking, incredibly profound, and well-considered: "Now a slave has no permanent standing in the household, but a son belongs to it forever" (John 8:35). What this expression means is that as long as we are still slaves to our own labor, we don't abide. The Son abides in the house of truth, which is pure transparency: everything has become transparent. In the house there is stability, continuity, rest, security, and reciprocity. In our finiteness and relativity, in our actual form, we feel encompassed, held, loved, and desired by what we might call the Principle of the Unconditional. In this way, we can see that the word "abiding," even though it is well known, still can represent a wealth of experiences that we can try and trace so we can find out what exactly is going to happen in the process we have embarked upon. Our hope is that movement and rest will finally coincide—movement, freed from strain and great difficulty; and rest, full of dynamic power and spontaneity.

* * *

"Do Not Judge"

"And the judgment is this...the light has come into the world" (John 3:19). This declaration of Jesus is one we have heard very often, but we don't realize how paradoxical it is. The phrase is linked with a command from Jesus from the synoptic gospels that strikes us as familiar: "Do not judge" (Matt. 7:1; Luke 6:37). Included here is the phrase "do not condemn."

We have already discussed judgment and its relationship with the intellect, but I now want to turn my attention to how we judge: in short, the role of light. We depend on light to perceive things. When observing a landscape for example, it makes a difference if it is light or dark, if the sun is shining or it is cloudy, or where the sun is positioned. The source of light determines what we see. So, while discernment and judgment may be functions of the mind, the source of light is essential to those faculties. Jesus' command "do not judge" effectively says: Do not affix your observation or judgment; be conscious of the fact that what you see and judge is defined by the source of light. There is an external source of light (the sun, the light), but there is also an inner source—the light we carry within us.

The concept "do not judge" is reinforced when it takes on the meaning of "do not condemn." Condemnation takes place when there's a certain value at stake, when a verdict about good and evil resounds in the condemnation. Very often a verdict about good and evil is not balanced and rational but stems from emotion. As I indicated earlier, all of us are well aware of the many emotional factors that play a role in our judgment. We often condemn someone just because we don't like them. When we evaluate people in our personal relationships the same thing occurs: as a result of emotional motives someone is pasted with a value-judgment. Indeed, judgment and condemnation as activities of the mind are influenced by a great deal of emotion. As such, the activities of our mind and our emotions are expressions of our small, restricted "I." Therefore, Jesus' assertion not to judge or condemn is actually a statement that desires to break through the "I" that is focused on its limited, confined self.

That is why the pronouncement of Jesus is so special. The real judgment is the light itself and not the activity of the mind, which restricts and draws boundaries. When Jesus declares that He has not come to judge (John 12:47), it is not his intention that everything stays vague, gets confused, and is allowed to merge so that nothing will be distinct, or inherently singular or valuable. His intention and the result are that we unfold our mind, and learn to judge, distinguish, and perceive a difference in value. More importantly, there is another step here. It is the step by which we break through the static, judgmental quality of our discriminating powers. We must learn to perceive value judgments as transient—especially when it comes to condemnation and the attachment of value judgments by which we write off someone else, push them away, or mark them as bad, insignificant, or dangerous. We must learn to see the relativity of those judgments and place them within the light that transcends us, the light that is the final reality.

God is light (John 1:5). The Father, the Origin, the very First and Ultimate is brightness, shining light. "The Father...shows us everything He Himself does" (John 5:20), without reservation. But when we judge, we fasten a value and ultimately become blind to that light. That is why Jesus says:

> It is for judgment that I have come into this world, so
> that those without sight may see and those with sight may
> become blind. (John 9:39)

In that binding of judgment we make ourselves blind. When we enter the silence of meditation, it seems as if all sorts of judgments exist within our consciousness, judgments with an imperative, definitive character. At stake here is our judgment of others, underneath which our condemnation is often concealed, our writing off of ourselves.

The stillness of meditation is not a confused, gray muddle. It is filled with apprehension, since judgment provokes apprehension. When people who need to decide and make a judgment do so, apprehension arises. In meditation, too, we must make a choice and take a decision—namely the surrender of our thoughts, the judgments, through which we open ourselves to the light. In this way, the significance of judging is totally reversed: the judgment is no longer a condemnation of either our fellow man or ourselves (i.e. "I am bad, I will do it wrong anyway, I cannot do it right"). Our self-judgment is broken when we come to stand in the ultimate light: "And the judgment is this...the light has come into the world" (John 3:19).

Our entire being, our whole essence comes to stand in that final light. Are we prepared to enter that light, to break through that small self-labeled world? Light has no boundaries, is infinite, and in our innermost essence we are destined for that light. We exist to receive the light and irradiate it again—even if only in a limited way, since we are limited beings. But the limited is, however, simultaneously and fundamentally receptive to the Infinite. This way the finite and limited may emanate the light and become a vessel for the pure, infinite luminescence.

I Am (John 8:28)

"I am" are the words of Jesus in the Gospel of Saint John—where they are repeated at least twice, in their full explosiveness (John 8: 28, 58). In saying "'I am," Jesus takes on the name of God from the Old Testament.

It is an assertion we can understand in two ways. On the one hand, the word "am," from the verb "to be," is absorbed in the "I": this is the height of narcissism. On the other hand, however, this might also be a question of the exact opposite: the "I" is absorbed into being. It is clear that all those remarks of Jesus in the Gospel of John concerning death and the "not-I" must be understood as the "I" being absorbed into being. If the latter is the case, then the assertion "I am" is one of the most dizzying statements you can imagine: "I am"—where the "I" is completely dissolved into "being." It's an assertion that doesn't allow us to complain of vertigo or agoraphobia! It implies we must take the plunge in the total loss of self. Our anxiety makes us cling to the "I" in the ultimate paradox: "I" is the condition for being and consciousness; but "I" is at the same time an immense barrier to being and awareness.

Herein, to reiterate, lies the whole struggle of meditation: to get from the "small I" to the "larger I." The trouble is located in the colossal fear we have in relinquishing our "I." In the Gospel of John, this fear is often associated with the group, the people around you whom you need in order to exist. "Why do people have no faith at all?" John effectively asks, answering that they seek praise and acknowledgment from the group (John 12:43). And, because of this fear, we are unable to take the plunge and consequently do not emerge at our innermost selves.

Why we don't do this is perhaps because we aggressively seek praise or stature and desire to be the center of it all. We might have a question of a dependent or obtrusive self-image. But in any case, it's always a question of that narcissistic self-image I need to exist that will always play a part. The "I" is the center of that consciousness, and in everything I do I remain conscious of the fact that I am doing it, feeling it, enduring it, and experiencing it. Constantly, I remain aware that "I is I." And that makes me the pivot, the narcissistic center of my experience.

We have to pass through fear to relinquish this. Fear seems to be something dreadful, and indeed it is. Yet, we sometimes hold on to our fears, depressions, and doubts, and even cultivate them, if only because they are an expression of the "I." If we are frightened, we at least have something!

How do we become receptive to the overwhelming character of being? This is a question that continuously darts through the mind during meditation. When we are seated the whole day, we are constantly occupied with our bearing, posture, manner of breathing, and the way we tune in to our consciousness. What matters, as I have noted before, is a continuous refinement of attention, a continuous dedication. But, in that sense of dedication, the "I" is playing a part again. And this way the intention for refinement, and purification of our attention, brings about a reinforcement of the "I."

How do we get into the movement of selflessness? The short answer is that we notice it of our own accord. When we stay revolving around ourselves, even if we intend to meditate actively, we observe the movement, as it were, grinding to a halt. In objectless awareness, however, there actually occurs an intensification of movement and an amplification or strengthening of consciousness. This is not an extinguishing or loss of awareness; but it is only possible when the "I" is being relinquished. This action requires an enormous refinement of attention, in which a great force is simultaneously developed. In the act we may experience an expansion and some kind of wholeness. The act of letting go of the "small I" so we can enter that great all-embracing universe of being is a breathtaking, dazzling, jump on life and death. When we do this, concealed in the present, there is the force of "being," a force that burns away all fear, doubt, discouragement, and awakens a fire in us, the fire of "being." "I am" is an assertion that holds a radical invitation, a great promise!

Step by step, that miracle and wonder can happen to us: "I am."

"I Am the Bread of Life" (John 6:35, 48)

In the Gospel of John, "I am" is marked in several different ways. Among these is Jesus' pronouncement: "I am the bread of life" (John 6:35, 48). This symbol makes us recognize a certain affixed aspect of our "I," which we saw needs to be stretched through the process of dying and through silence into the infinite boundlessness of being.

What is meant by the idea of "bread"? Bread is a symbol of want. The word itself makes us recognize that we are creatures of want. In addition to the aspects of judging and anxiety, need is a profound aspect of our "I," an innermost dimension of our experience. We are creatures of want. This is evident, for example, in our fantasies and in the images that pass through us silently. Sometimes we feel like a baby or small child who wants to be cherished or cuddled. We all are needy creatures and want to be lost in the singularity of being held and being loved, to be a unity in which our own emptiness is filled.

Yet, meditation is not a question of denial, but merely of finding the most profound purpose of something. Silence and emptiness do not signify denial, but point to a process of transformation. At the beginning of the process we may already suspect or sense something of the ultimate toward which we are heading. What matters is that we are "stretched," lifted beyond ourselves, transformed, or "formed-over" (to use Jan van Ruysbroek's term). For "bread" is really not only a symbol of the want that makes us feel the pain of our frustrations, disappointments, and the emptiness through which we are thrown back upon ourselves. "Bread" has also the significance of the ultimate, a meaning of mutual sharing. Bread as a symbol shows us that we are dependent on each other, that we are thrown back on each other's company. Sometimes we feel how relationships form a cocoon around us, how the pattern of relationships continuously throws us back on ourselves, and how these patterns often express themselves in self-pity. But, the ultimate significance of bread is to learn to give ourselves to each other and to communicate with each other. This is a process in which something is continuously purified, clarified, and elucidated.

What is our relationship with other people? Do we constantly fire daggers at each other? Does everything revolve around that "small I"? Is everything interpreted only in so far as our desires are gratified and nothing else? Or are we turned toward the other and are we conscious that, in that symbol of bread, we exist for the other, in the sort of total mutual dependence that determines our humanity?

This dependence is revealed when we look at the different stages that have to be passed through if the wheat is to become bread. All these stages are full of rich symbolism. We humans, who are the grain in the flour, dissolve in the flour. Similarly, we must die to our "I," which throws us back on ourselves. Leaven or yeast is the force that makes the dough rise. That way we may experience, in stillness, the mysterious force that opens us to a new universe, admitting new dimensions. The dough must be baked in the oven. We are purified by fire, because fire has the significance of sacrifice and self-bestowal. Similarly, the process of silence is not for ourselves. To the contrary, silence wants to open us out to the world and humanity. It wants us to unfold everything in total love, compassion, and solidarity. That way our self-focused need is converted and transformed into self-bestowal and compassion.

Sitting together in meditation reflects standing around the altar. We form a circle. That circle points to solidarity, warmth, and security. The altar and the silence in the hall of meditation both point to the singular process that each and every one of us has to pass through alone, and which, however close we might get to each other, cannot be taken over from each other. The purpose of the singular process of going through the Great Death is the bestowal of self to each other, in compassion and love.

❦